THE **V** FOUNDATION®
for Cancer Research

In 1983, Jim Valvano led North Carolina State to a National Title. In June of 1992, Jim was diagnosed with terminal cancer and nearly one year later, passed away at the age of 47. No one can forget the passion that Jimmie V had for life. During one of his final interviews he stated, "I want to help every cancer patient I can now. I don't know if I can handle that, but it's the only conceivable good that can come out of this."

In Jim Valvano's memory, The V Foundation was formed, and today serves as a charitable organization dedicated to saving lives by helping to find a cure for cancer. The foundation seeks to make a difference by generating broad-based support for cancer research and by creating an urgent awareness among all Americans of the importance of the fight against cancer.

A portion of the proceeds from *Teammates Matter* will go directly to the V Foundation. For more information, please contact 1–800–4JIMMYV or email info@jimmyv.org

"DON'T GIVE UP ... DON'T EVER GIVE UP!" ®

Endorsements for Alan Williams & *Teammates Matter*:

"At a young age, Alan has a great ability to communicate his message of perseverance, while emphasizing the importance of teamwork. His commitment to hard work and his determination to stay a part of the team tell a very inspirational story that all young people should have a chance to hear."

Allen L. Shiver
President
Flowers Foods, Inc.

"In the midst of a sports-obsessed culture, Alan Williams restores a sense of proportion and perspective gleaned from his experience as a walk-on at Wake Forest. His is a heartfelt, grace-saturated story that does not sugarcoat reality; instead he conveys the pain and heartache, the disappointment and sacrifice, and ultimately the joy and fulfillment of being a part of something larger than self: the enduring perspective of a 'team-mate.' Alan's message resonates with folks as old as 7 and as young as 7x7."

Steve Collums (1950–2009)
Longtime Educator & Administrator
Memphis, Tennessee

TEAMMATES MATTER.

FIGHTING FOR SOMETHING GREATER THAN SELF

ALAN WILLIAMS

NEW HEIGHTS PRESS

To my Amanda—the best teammate I will ever have.

teammates matter.™

™

Contents

HALFTIME: DON'T GIVE UP

SECOND HALF: WALK-ON

TEAM MEETING: MUCH MORE THAN A GAME

THE LOCKER ROOM: TEAMMATES

PRESS CONFERENCE: FINISHING THE RACE

MORNING PAPER: REFLECTIONS

TEAMMATES MATTER.

SCOUTING REPORT
Big Dreams

*E*very year before the season would start, Coach would gather us all in a huddle. With a basketball in his right hand, he would say, "Fellas, enjoy going to the gym . . . enjoy working hard . . . enjoy all there is to enjoy about the game we love because one day no matter who you are—no matter how many points you score or how good of a career you have . . . one day, the ball will stop bouncing."

With chills running down my arms, I would watch each time as Coach would drop the basketball he was holding—it would bounce three or four times.

Then, in a quiet moment, my teammates and I would stare at the ball now resting on the ground.

Walk-on, *n.* someone who plays a sport in college without an athletic scholarship.

1

Fighting for Something Greater than Self

MY NAME really isn't all that important. Buddy will do—that's what they called me:

"Buddy, you're better than that."

"Buddy, go rebound for those guys."

"Y'all take Buddy on your team."

I was Buddy. I was #20, a 6′2″, 175-pound shooting guard from Memphis, Tennessee. During my collegiate career, I averaged 7 points, 3 rebounds, and 4 assists *per year*. In 120 games, I played only 59 minutes. "Above the rim" meant nothing to me.

I was a walk-on. I never got a scholarship to play Division One basketball, so I didn't know what it was like to answer questions at a press conference. I didn't know what it was like to hit a game-winning shot. And I didn't know what it was like to be hounded by little kids for autographs. The reality of the matter is I was the guy who loved the game; the teammate who went crazy on the bench; and the one player you looked at from the stands and said, "I can take him!" When I checked into the game, the fans knew it was time to get a head start to the car to beat the traffic. And yes, I was the one player on my team that couldn't dunk; occasionally I slapped the backboard on the way in for a lay-up.

I know you've seen the portrayal of major college sports from plenty of stars, but let me give you a different look—a perspective where playing time and glamour are minimal. I've played for two highly respected coaches and been to four NCAA Tournaments. You've probably never seen me on ESPN, but you've also never heard my story nor the story of big time hoops from the angle of the one player on the team who sees everything—the walk-on.

Some of my statistics only I know. I went 16-16 in warm-ups against Kansas, but if you go to the record books, you won't find any documentation of that feat. Thankfully, my experience at Wake Forest went beyond mere numbers. For that reason, the destination of this story is not a heroic moment where I was carried off the court to thousands of screaming fans. Had this been the case, it might suggest that only an outcome leading to *15 seconds of fame* could somehow make all my hard work and sacrifice worthwhile—that would be an injustice to what I consider to be the true *success* of any story.

The roller coaster journey of being a walk-on was one of the most rewarding, yet humbling, experiences of my life. Even though I was a part of one of the most celebrated basketball conferences in the country, unavoidable challenges came along with being a walk-on. I know not everyone is an athlete, but I believe that we've all had times in our lives when we feel like we're sitting on the end of the bench—whatever our "bench" happened to be.

Now, don't count me out if you happen to feel like the star or if your role on your team doesn't coincide with the sentiments I've expressed in these first few pages. I've played with, roomed with, and carefully observed plenty of stars whose impact on my life will be worth noting whether you're the starter, the sixth man, or the practice player. In high school, I still remember what it was like to feel like the star and score *all of the points*, but as it turns out, my faith and my ability to confront adversity were put to the test more frequently when my seat on the bench was farthest from the coach.

I recognize that if the point of this book hinges on me 'sitting on the end of the bench' then there would be no reason to keep reading because any successful team cannot afford to have players who *just* sit on the sidelines—our ACC Championship team was no exception. There was no room for any player one through fifteen who did not contribute and find value in his role.

At one point during my career, a reporter approached me from the *Greensboro News and Record.* He was writing an article that focused on walk-ons in the ACC. He asked me, "Alan, you hardly ever played, you hardly ever scored—why did you fight so hard to be on this team?"

Keep in mind, I had never been interviewed by the media in college. While my answers to these questions may have satisfied the reporter and led to decent quotes in the next day's morning paper, I remained perplexed and unsatisfied with my responses. "Why did I fight so hard to be a part of this team? Why was it worth it? And what made it successful?" The deepest corners of my heart needed to know.

My junior year, we had just beaten North Carolina at Chapel Hill and were traveling westbound on Interstate 40 back to Winston-Salem. Everyone had fallen asleep at the back of the bus that night, but me. Quietly, I flipped to an old notebook, found an empty page, and began to write. These are my thoughts.

2

Love The Game

"Oᴋ, there's 10 seconds to go, we're down two . . . the ball is at half court. Let's go for the tie; the pick'n roll has been working all night."

"But Coach, we're on the road, we gotta go for the win," I exclaimed as I began tapping my head profusely.

Tap the head was the signal we used for the *picket fence*—a play we only ran during end of game situations—a play that ended with me shooting a three near the top of the key. Now was the perfect time.

Coach finally gave in, *tap the head* it was. With my sweatband halfway up my arm *like Mike*, I came out of the timeout with a swagger you couldn't buy at the mall.

"Come on, Alan."

"You got this."

"Play your game."

"Relax."

"Be ready to shoot."

Before I knew it, our *veteran point guard* was dribbling the ball up the right side of the floor, all the while tapping his head.

"10, 9, 8, 7, 6."

Hovering in the middle of the lane, I took a few steps towards the right corner, but then immediately made a sharp v-cut back across the lane up towards *the picket fence* waiting for me near the top of the key.

"5, 4, 3 . . ."

With my hands ready, I rubbed tight off of the screen like I was supposed to, caught the pass, squared my feet and......knocked it down...nothing but net!

As an 11-year-old having seen too many NBA highlights, I backpedaled down the court with a look on my face that basically said, "I told you so." Oh, and my follow through; don't worry, it was still high in the air.

During the aftermath of it all, I was a little disappointed to look at the bleachers and be reminded that the fans must have decided to sleep in that Saturday morning, thus, missing out on the action at the local high school gym. With a sigh of relief, though, I looked back towards the opposite end of the court where I saw and heard the only reaction I needed. The only other person in the gym besides me was signaling with his hands above his head that the three-pointer had been made. It was my Dad— *the wavering coach, the veteran point guard,* and *the shot clock* all in one.

As for the *picket fence* near the top of the key—a trash can coupled with the imagination of a fifth grader and a father who gladly played along did the job just fine.

Later in my career, fictitious scenarios like these would become reality, and I would continually find myself in pressure-filled situations. The magnitude of this pressure seemed to increase as I got older. More fans, bigger gyms, established rivalries, and greater expectations made the rim seem a little smaller when attempting to make two clutch free throws.

Before each game I played in high school, I made a point to remember those times in the gym with my Dad where the basket seemed bigger than ever. With that nervous feeling churning inside my stomach at my locker, I would pray for a youthful mindset and sometimes even tell myself,

"Alan, tonight play like you're ten years old in the backyard." Just telling myself to be a certain way didn't necessarily work, but I knew that my game would be at its best if I could combine my skills with certain child-like tendencies. Of course, I'm not referring to a young player's competence in understanding the high post offense. I'm talking about a love for the game, a fearless spirit, and a stubbornness that thinks if you wear the same number Larry Bird wears, you'll play just like 'em.

One of my favorite movies was *The Pistol*. In the film, I'll never forget Pistol Pete Maravich explaining that he liked knowing that he would practice and get better at times when no one else was watching. For a time, I thought I was the Pistol, so I not only slept with my basketball, but also refused to let anyone outwork me.

I loved the details of the game. My t-shirt used to say *Basketball is Life . . . the rest is just details*. Not exactly a sermon title, but this exaggeration reminds me that there is so much more to loving the game than just putting the ball through the hoop. The cold winter air, NCAA Tournament theme music, the smell of the visitor's locker room, dimly lit gyms; all of these elements not only ignited a passion for basketball, but also started the journey I'm reflecting on.

In junior high school, I played for a competitive traveling team and before games, our coach, a local doctor in town, would unwrap two Hershey's chocolate bars in the locker room. One by one, Dr. Snyder would hand each of us a small rectangular piece of the chocolate. He claimed it would give us more energy—I believed him.

Unfortunately, this youthful energy is sometimes sapped by a culture that promotes individualism over team, *coolness* instead of hustle, and acting *like you've been there before* as opposed to savoring each moment.

As time went on, I naturally wanted more than just a small piece of the chocolate. I wanted the whole Hershey's bar. Perhaps that could be considered a weakness or a strength, but I hope that I never lose the ability to make a big deal out of little things or find joy in small victories as we did in the days of celebrating every win with a pizza party. Focusing on the moment that is here and not the moment I'm waiting for, playing to win and not to lose, expecting the best and not the worst—all little lessons from our youth that us big people sometimes forget.

As you can probably tell, I was not a first-round draft choice in the NBA. While many of my dreams as a kid have been replaced with reality, there is always room to dream new dreams.

March 1995

As a confident seventh grader, my dreams were big and only got bigger as I found myself watching the 1995 ACC Championship game. As I finished the last bites of my hot dog, the TV revealed the frustration behind the stoic face of North Carolina coach Dean Smith as Randolph Childress of Wake Forest hit a demoralizing shot with only four seconds left in the game—one of several crucial baskets that propelled the Demon Deacons to their first ACC Tournament title since 1962. Minutes later, I marveled as I watched Childress and his first-team All-American teammate Tim Duncan celebrate the unforgettable history they had just made.

As the players began to climb the ladder to cut down the nets, I wondered if I would ever have a chance to play for a program like Wake Forest. I recalled the list my dad and I had compiled on the way to basketball camp the previous summer. The list consisted of the schools I dreamed of getting a scholarship from, and Wake was number one.

The images I had of Duncan and others cutting the nets could not escape me. I wanted to play for Wake Forest. I wanted to play in places like the Dean Dome and Cameron Indoor Stadium. I wanted to wear the same perfectly white Nike shoes Tim Duncan wore. I wanted to play college basketball in the ACC!

August 2000

Since Tim Duncan won his second ACC Championship that spring in 1995, his life had undergone significant changes. He was the number one pick in the 1997 NBA Draft and later became the Rookie of the Year in 1998. In only his second season with the San Antonio Spurs, Duncan won a championship and received Most Valuable Player honors.

How do you go from where you are to where you want to be? I think you have to have an enthusiasm for life. You have to have a dream, a goal, and you have to be willing to work for it.

—JIM VALVANO

In the fall of 2000, while working through a summer injury, Duncan made his way to Winston-Salem to receive an award at the halftime of a Wake Forest football game. In addition to accepting his award, Duncan made a concerted effort to join members of the current Wake basketball team for some pickup games.

Just as Tim Duncan's life had changed since I watched him in the ACC Tournament back in junior high, my life, though less televised, had changed as well. This was especially true on a Saturday in September of my freshman year of college, when I found myself in Reynolds Gymnasium carefully tying my shoes. A random guy sat down next to me and said, "What's up, man?" I tugged at my shoe strings, looked up, and nodded my head, replying, "Hey man." Then I quickly, but coolly, looked back down at my shoes, tugged at my strings even harder this time, and thought, *How in the world am I lacing up my shoes next to Tim Duncan?*

Maybe I'll let him play on my team.

3

Garf

HOWARD GARFINKLE is one of the most renowned figures in all of basketball. He was the director of the famed Five-Star Basketball Camp, which, for more than four decades, has showcased some of the nation's top high school recruits. Over the years, his camp has produced over 320 NBA players.

To understand the true character of Garf, as he is affectionately known, one must consider the passion he has for a game whose purpose is often misunderstood. With Garf setting the tone, Five-Star breeds a brand of basketball that is predicated on a genuine respect for the traditions of a sport meant to be played purely. At his camp, it wasn't about the logo on your shoes, but about learning the fundamentals of the game while having an opportunity to gain exposure from college coaches.

Any camp can divide up all of the players and play five-on-five from sunup to sundown, but Five-Star took a different approach:

a daily schedule that did not discount the importance of teaching a camper how to effectively handle a half-court trap or properly set up a defender before using a screen.

Garf was unique and, despite being in his 70s at the time and still sporting yellow pants, he had a knack for corralling some of the nation's best talent at his camps each summer.

Years ago, it was reported that Garf was standing outside an NBA arena near the players' entrance when he began to frantically yell as he saw one of his former campers, then a pro, making his way into the arena. Unfortunately for Garf, security was extremely tight, and his efforts to get the player's attention were thwarted by the officials supervising the area.

Garf remained persistent though. Unabashedly, he yelled for the player as he tried to cross under the ropes but was again detained by the police, since he lacked the necessary credentials to proceed through. Before the professional player crossed the threshold of the door, however, his head began to turn: he recognized the distinct and unforgettable voice. Without hesitation, the player looked, pointed at the security guards, and said, "If it weren't for that man right there, I wouldn't be here. He's coming with me." Garf then crossed under the ropes with more than enough credentials—and together, he and Michael Jordan proceeded into the arena.

When it comes to basketball, the total opposite of Michael Jordan is Alan Williams; but like Mike, I owe much to Garf. I can honestly say that if it weren't for Howard Garfinkle I wouldn't have played basketball at Wake Forest University.

The summer after my sophomore year of high school, I attended the Pittsburgh session of Five-Star at Robert Morris College. It was the hottest part of the afternoon on court 3. I was having an okay game; but due to my offensively eager teammates, I was having trouble getting open shots. After figuring out that nobody was going to spot me up for a jumper, I decided to get more aggressive. Four straight times down the court I made a move on my man, pulled up, and scored. Since I was 6'2" and vertically challenged, I knew I couldn't get to the rim very often. I had to pull-up.

In an era of basketball in which the midrange game is a lost art, I perfected it for a three-minute period on the blacktop that hot July afternoon. Fortunately, Howard Garfinkle was watching. Out of the twenty games going on in camp, Garf happened to be gazing through the holes of the fence behind court 3. Not knowing my name, he approached me after the game, sat down next to me, and said with his New York accent, "That was some good *stuff* out there. What's your name kid? I like your handles. Can you shoot it? You got the grades?"

I answered affirmatively to his questions, and that's when he told me he wanted me to be sure and come back the next summer. He said, "You can play, son."

One year later, I returned to Five-Star for two more weeks of camp. During these sessions, out of the corner of my eye, I would see Garf escort coaches from schools like Davidson, Brown, and Navy over to my court. He would point, and of course, I pretended not to see these things as I dived after loose balls and yelled, "I got weak side help," "I got your help," or "BALL, BALL, BALL!"

Along the way, Garf promised there would be a place for me at a good school. However, in the fall of my senior year, my choices were limited. Oh yeah, and my big dream of Wake Forest was not even in the picture. I had come to grips that there was no way I was good enough to get a scholarship in the ACC. While there were a number of low-major and mid-major colleges that requested official visits and home visits, I was intent on being at a school I would want to attend even if I didn't play basketball.

One day I picked up the phone at my house. Surprisingly, it was Howard Garfinkle calling to ask me how the recruiting process was going. I was not exactly the most prized recruit at his camp the past summer, so I was shocked he was calling me. Displaying frustration, I informed him I had not found the right school yet. That's when he said, "Well, would you ever want to walk on?"

"Yes, sir," I said, "but if I do that, I want to attend a school with a great combination of academics and basketball."

"Well, I'm going to watch Wake Forest play at Virginia tomorrow," he said. "I'll go talk to Davey Odom and tell him a little bit about you. Don't worry though—I'll take care of you."

Did he say WAKE FOREST?

To be honest, I don't know exactly what transpired that next night in Charlottesville, Virginia. But I do know that three weeks later I was in a room with my dad and Lee Smith, my high school coach, on a conference call with the coach of Wake Forest, Dave Odom. He assured me I could come to Wake and be a guaranteed walk-on for four years.

On March 5, 2000, after eating a piece of my mom's celebration cake with black and gold icing, I signed an official letter of intent to attend the number one school on my list from years ago. Sure, it wasn't a scholarship, but it was still Wake Forest—I was headed for Winston-Salem, North Carolina.

You can learn a lot about a man by the promises
he keeps in small conversation.

—BOWMAN WILLIAMS, MY DAD.

Two years before at Five-Star, I had played awesome for three minutes and three minutes alone. Garf happened to be watching all three. Fortunately, this wouldn't be the last time he would look after me. I don't believe in coincidences—only in God's timing.

In the years to come, I'll be watching ESPN: the announcers, as always, will point out the famed Five-Star director and all the great players that have come through his camp. I will see him, smile and know that I was never a Michael Jordan or a LeBron James; I was just Alan Williams, and a man chose to take an interest in me that no one else was willing to take.

As you might guess, I will never walk through a players' entrance to an NBA arena—I never got drafted. However, should Howard Garfinkle ever run into trouble getting into one of my church-league games when I'm thirty, I'll be sure and say, "That guy is with me."

WARM-UPS
Freshman Trials

I was a freshman in study hall. Between fervent attempts to begin studying, some of the scholarship players began to give another teammate a hard time, flippantly poking fun at how much time he had been spending with his new girlfriend. It seemed harmless at the moment, so I decided to throw in my two cents. While I found that my contributions yielded temporarily rewarding laughter from much of the room, it was only a matter of time before I saw a noticeably large fist coming in the direction of my face.

It hurt. That night in study hall, I came to the conclusion that, as a freshman walk-on, I wasn't allowed to joke around with our seven-foot center from Germany just yet.

4

Weight Room

Sweat accumulated in a small puddle below me as I tried to make it through the drill.

"Down!"

"Up!"

"Down! Stay down—you're not getting any better if you don't stay down."

"That's seven; three more!"

"Buddy, don't lose me here!"

"Down!...Up!...That's eight, boys!"

I was trying with all my might to keep my arms locked, but something inside me knew my body was not doing what my mind was telling me I could do.

Ervin Murray, my partner, yelled in my ear as he straightened the 55-pound plate that lay on top of my back, "Buddy, you got this. Don't you quit, don't you quit. Knock this out, boy!"

"Down!"

I unlocked my arms to go down for the eighth push-up.

Plop!

My arms gave out on me. I sat up on my knees, angrily gasping for a breath of air as I looked at my teammates around me—now on their ninth pushup, holding it with perfect form. "Come on, Buddy, you're better than that," the strength coach said. I was mad. I got back down on the ground and told Ervin to put the red plate on my back for the last two push-ups.

I pushed off the ground, but I had no feeling in my arms and dropped straight to the floor. I became even more frustrated. That's when Ervin said, "Here, let me take this weighted plate off ...now try." After Ervin took the 55 pounds off my back, I unlocked my arms again. This time, I was able to go down and hold the last push-up. "Good job, Buddy."

"Up...good job, fellas. That's ten. Buddy, keep gettin' better. Huddle up, fellas...we'll see you tomorrow."

We all put our hands in the huddle.

"1...2...3...WAKE!"

That was my welcome to Wake Forest. We ended every upper body workout with push-ups that year. Every time I heard the strength coach say, "Get a partner, get a red plate: push-ups. Let's go boys," I cringed.

Weights and conditioning that fall marked the beginning of a long struggle. Maybe I couldn't do everything as well as the other guys, but I worked my tail off. Once a week, we woke up at 5:45 A.M. to run a three-mile route around campus. Attendance was mandatory. Coach Odom loved to run; he made the whole team—the coaches, the managers, and even the trainers—participate. I actually handled the distance aspect of these workouts with ease. I frequently finished first in the mileage, but when we crossed over to agility and sprints, I was clearly at a disadvantage.

Although I was never going to beat anyone in a footrace, that freshman year I worked as hard as any player on that team.

I vividly remember being on the football field on Sunday nights running suicides. Sprinting to the 20 yard line and back, 40 and back, 60 and back, 80 and back, and 100 and back in a minute and a half was no easy task, but I embraced the challenge—so much so that some of my teammates didn't like it.

"Buddy's working. Way to go, Buddy," the coach would say.

I suppose part of me knew that I had to work to make up for my fall-outs in the weight room, so I tried harder than the other guys. In turn, they would say things like, "Calm down, Buddy." Another would say, "The season hasn't started yet, dawg."

If I cool it, I won't help you guys
get ready for the next week's game!

—RUDY

We did slides across the width of the lane in the gym. "Thirty seconds, ready, GO!" I went as fast as I possibly could. My shirt was drenched in sweat. I could hear some of the guys in line chuckling, saying, "This man's crazy!" I wasn't going any faster than any of the other guys. I was going at the same pace, but I had to exert so much more energy in order to keep up—my beet-red face and lathered shirt showed it. It was always humbling finishing my slides and going back to the end of the line, where I had to watch my teammates smoothly and swiftly slide across the lane with ease and even occasional smiles on their faces. In other words, I had to use all of my hustle to match what they would call "coasting." What came easy to the scholarship guys was always difficult for me.

Unfortunately, the laughs that followed my defensive slides were not the only laughs directed my way that fall. Toward the end of the preseason we had an event called "Run with the Deacs." It was a fundraiser for Brian Piccolo Cancer Research, where people would pay $15 to run a 5K race with the basketball team. The event was significant because it was the first time the team was seen in public. All the media cameras and newspaper writers were in attendance, so Coach Odom was sure to request a decent effort.

I took off from the starting line like a shot out of a cannon knowing in the back of my mind I could finish before all of the other guys. That was where my problem began. As the local runners with short shorts passed me, I kept a solid pace and proceeded along the cross-country course that weaved through the woods on the outer edge of campus. Twenty-two minutes later, I came out of the clearing in the woods and approached the finish line. The large clock in the distance revealed a reasonable time. As I ran the final straightaway, I couldn't help but be proud of the fact I was the first of my teammates to finish.

As I crossed the finish line, all of the bystanders began to clap, at which time I received a much needed cup of Gatorade. Seconds later, as I continued walking through the crowd, I couldn't help but notice Craig Dawson, Broderick Hicks, Antwan Scott, and the rest of my team all sitting down on benches off to the side, not a drop of sweat on their bodies.

"Buddy, why is your face so red, dawg?"

It was so red because I had run the race I thought I was

supposed to run, while they had cut through the woods. I felt stupid. I was humiliated. I wasn't used to cutting corners in life, and it was hard to be ridiculed for not knowing the ropes like the other players.

Don't get me wrong. I had plenty of meals and good times with my teammates that fall, but I was tired of being a target for an easy laugh.

One day, I asked an assistant coach where I could get running shoes like everyone else. That's when Ernie Nestor, the top assistant, told me, "You'll have to ask Sarge. He deals with all that stuff. Oh, and good luck!"

"What's that supposed to mean?" I asked, still showing my newcomer naivete. Apparently, Sarge was our equipment manager and he was known for sometimes not liking walk-ons.

I went back to the other walk-on, Matt (or "Woody," as he was called), and told him we would have to ask Sarge about our shoes. We were taking pictures for the media guide that day, so I knew we would run into him at the photo shoot later in the afternoon. Sure enough, Matt and I walked over to the athletic center and watched as all the players tried to look tough for the cover of the media guide.

The photographer even had a spray bottle to make some of the players look bigger than they really were. I definitely could have used a little spray-bottle action on my body, but Matt and I, of course, were not provided jerseys to take the pictures in the first place. In light of yet another setback, we still decided to go to Sarge and ask him where we could get the running shoes. His response was clear and unforgettable: "There is a Foot Locker at Hanes Mall around the corner."

Coach Odom approached me in the weight room one day. I

can still remember him saying, "Are you enjoying this? Is every-thing going like you thought it would, Alan?"

NO, NO, NO! I thought, but I still answered affirmatively because I refused to give in. I thought I was being tested by every-one in the program, so I refused to forfeit my pride. I was emo-tionally drained, though, and could feel the frustrations penetrating deeper and deeper into my heart. For the first time in my life, I didn't measure up on the basketball court. I had gone from being the guy in high school who takes twenty shots a game to being the guy whose teammates tell him not to shoot.

Never in my life had I been anxious about having to do a push-up or run a suicide. Constantly, I feared being the one that would have to make the whole team run all over again. I was doing everything I could to get better: I was eating more than I ever had, running extra miles, shooting at night, coming in on off days, doing push-ups in my dorm, and drinking protein shakes every night. I loved being on the team, but I had never before been the *last* guy on the team—the *smallest*, the *slowest*, and the *weakest*.

5

Travel Bag

"Yes, is Robert there?"

"No, he's out with his father right now, can I take a message?"

"Sure, this is Alan Williams."

"Who?"

"This is Alan Williams. I'm gonna be playing for Wake Forest this fall and was trying to get in touch with Robert."

"Oh, okay, Alan, I'll tell Rob you called."

You have no idea how much courage it took to pick up the phone and call Robert O'Kelley that summer before my freshman year. He was Wake Forest's marquee player at the time, ACC Freshman of the Year, and of course, a local hero in our hometown, Memphis. I felt like I was trying to call up "the girl" . . . you know, when you only dial six digits and then hang up. Rob was the man, and I wanted a chance to work out with him before I made my way to Winston-Salem.

Robert promptly called me back. The next day I met him at his old high school to work out. I arrived thirty minutes early to warm up. After shooting for about fifteen minutes—all the while gazing at the O'Kelley jersey in the rafters—Rob walked in with his gold Nike dri-fit shirt and his Wake basketball shorts. This was the guy.

I remembered the time my Dad and I drove to Nashville to see him face off against Tony Harris (who later played for Tennessee) in the state championship. Harris and O'Kelley were the two most talked about athletes in Memphis during their high school careers. Every Saturday morning I opened the paper to see how well each of them had performed in the previous night's games.

I'll never forget the time in high school Robert reportedly slept through his alarm, arriving late to the game. Despite not getting to start, Robert still managed to pour in fifty-four points! He was a pure shooter, and Dick Vitale had been raving about him on ESPN for three years with words like, "Robert O'Kelley, he's awesome baby, AT&T long distance bomber, trifecta city!"

As Robert approached me in the gym the day of our workout, I was flustered because I didn't know what kind of handshake he was throwing at the time. There were options, but I didn't know which one to go with:

- a simple handshake.
- a dap (fist)
- a dap followed by two more daps, under and over
- a handshake ending in a snap
- a short handshake with a small hug.

I decided the simple handshake was too conventional. The dap was too impersonal. The dap with more daps was too complicated.

The hug was too "you're already my boy," but the handshake with the snap was perfect.

After the much anticipated clasping of the hands, we talked for a bit and then began to warm up. Rob went down to the other end of the court and started a one-handed progressive shooting drill. Watching him on TV, I thought of Rob only as a star, so I was amazed at how humble he was: his voice and everything about the way he presented himself.

Since I was in "date mode," I, of course, had already prepared some go-to questions if things got a little quiet. But I didn't even get a chance to ask them, because he had already asked me about all my high school experiences, summer plans, and even my family.

Eventually we began the workout that Rob said would be comparable to the preseason workouts we would be doing that fall at Wake Forest. Shooting was the one thing I thought I could do really well. Although it was intense, I enjoyed it. That is until I realized we were *not* going to rest between reps and that our workout would last nearly an hour and a half—a clear indication of how serious the transition between high school and college would be.

Shooting workouts in college were like simulated games. The clock is on, the chairs are out, and you don't just step into your shot—you run from the baseline to half court, back to the three-point line, catch, controlled shot fake, two dribbles, rise and shoot. Do this routine until you make ten shots, and you will surely be gasping for breath. Intensity is expected though, and if you're not in shape, you won't make it through a workout.

After we finished shooting, we walked outside to our cars and exchanged phone numbers. How great it was to put Robert O'Kelley's name in my "celly," as my teammates called it. I had only known him two hours, and he was already treating me like a teammate.

The next day, we went to a community center to lift and get in a few pickup games. I always loved watching the little kids' faces as we passed. They would whisper, "There's Robert O'Kelley... whoa, it's really him!" And yes, I was the guy faithfully tagging along behind.

This particular day with Rob started in the weight room. It was a most memorable experience. You see, Rob was jacked. He had huge arms and a chest that was worthy of immediate respect. He had 3-percent body fat along with bulging veins. Rob was a first-class athlete and so strong the coaches wouldn't let him do the same workout the rest of the team did for fear it might mess up his touch.

On the other hand, I was barely busting out of my homemade cutoff gray t-shirt (if Rob wore one, so did I). I think I had one or two veins protrude above the surface of my skin when I did curls; but other than that, at 6'2", 169 pounds, I was not your prototype D-1 athlete. I'm sure Robert hated working out with me because I made him do two workouts. First, he pumped out his ten reps, and then had to take 200 pounds off the bar so that I could "get my lift on." It was all about the lingo, I'm telling you.

Those two days with Rob marked the beginning of our friendship. Freshman year, Rob was my only teammate that called me by my real name. He looked out for me, and I tried to work out with him as much as possible. Each Saturday morning before football games, we went through a series of shooting drills and ended with defensive slides. Robert was a tireless worker. He was the first guy at practice and the last to leave. The one year I played with Rob, I learned a lot about his work ethic, but I learned even more about his character.

After finishing conditioning and weights one day, the team was in the locker room. Sarge came in with a box of new Nike travel bags. They were huge bags with a perfectly embroidered WF, a sizable white Nike swoosh, and a label with each player's number. Keep in mind, gear was a major deal to all the players, and I couldn't wait to get mine so I could be that guy who excessively sported his gear around campus. As Sarge began to lay the bags at the foot of our lockers, I couldn't help but notice he skipped over mine. For whatever reason, I didn't get a bag. But of course I couldn't say anything because I was just a freshman walk-on trying to fit in.

I had been at every workout, lifted every weight, and run every mile. Why wasn't I getting a team bag? These were my thoughts as I stared at my old beat-up high school gym bag laying at the base of my locker. I was discouraged—and even more discouraged when Rafael Vidaurreta, a 6'10" center from Spain, walked by my locker and said softly in my ear, "Don't worry about it, dude. You already know Sarge doesn't like walk-ons." The rest of my teammates looked at me and saw the hurt in my eyes, but could only say things like, "That's messed up, dawg. You deserve to get the same *stuff* we get."

I didn't understand this. I was told I would be treated like a scholarship player. I was defenseless, though, and proceeded to the showers with the rest of the guys. As the hot water beat down on my head, I questioned whether or not I was going to be able to endure many more discouraging situations like this one. After a long shower, I went back into the locker area to dry off. By now, most of my teammates had left. While walking back to my stool, I observed all the lockers, each of which had a fancy, engraved sign with the player's name and number. I stopped at mine, the locker with an uneven piece of masking tape above it reading WILLIAMS #20.

I sat down on a stool and opened my locker. To my surprise, there was a WF travel bag—brand new, just like all the other guys'. At this point, I figured Sarge, knowing that I was disappointed, had come to grips with himself and decided to give me a bag of

---

Humility is not thinking less of yourself,
but thinking of yourself less.

—C. S. LEWIS

---

my own, but I realized this wasn't the case. As I carefully placed my shoes inside, I noticed the label on my bag. As I looked closer, I didn't see a #20, but a #4 instead.

Robert O'Kelley was #4.

Throughout freshman year, my teammates often gave me a hard time, referring to Robert as "Buddy's hero." Everyone knew I loved Rob, and maybe if they had seen the excitement on my face when I realized I had my very first travel bag, they would have understood why I respected him so much.

Rob was our leader—and he acted like it.

6

Open Gym

"Foul!"

"You know that ain't no foul."

"You trippin'. A foul is a foul. Check out my arm."

"C'mon, man, this ain't high school, dawg."

"Five to three, ball game. Let's play."

These were the sounds of pickup basketball during the preseason at Wake Forest. It was intense. Our team was close, but when we divided into two teams, a supportive environment turned into one full of competitive hostility.

My freshman year, the games were controlled by simple rules: first one to seven wins, everything counts as one point, call your own fouls, winner stays, losers off, next five on.

Going to Wake Forest, I knew that pickup, or "open gym" as we called it, was going to be a critical time, because it would be an opportunity to prove to the players I was worthy of being on their team. Coaches weren't allowed at open gym, so gaining my teammates' respect was paramount. I knew the coaches could love everything about my game; but if my teammates didn't approve of me, I should probably opt for intramurals.

Sean Tuohy, the all-time assists leader at Ole Miss, talked with my dad on the phone one day. Dad asked if he had any advice for me before I started working out with the Wake players that fall. He said, "Alan's a good shooter, but tell him to make sure not to shoot in pickup games. The best thing he can do to bond with the other players is to pass the ball. And if he does take a shot, he better make it because those guys will be all over him if he shoots too much."

I remember showing up to open gym for the very first time. As I shot around at the other end of the floor, the veteran guys slowly began to form the teams. Of course, no one begged for my services, so I had to wait for the next game. As I watched, I couldn't help but notice the size of these athletes. Craig Dawson was a two guard, 6'5", 205 pounds. Josh Howard, who now plays in the NBA, was 6'7", 210, and Josh Shoemaker, 6'10", 230. There is no need to remind you of my dimensions again, but I was more than just a little intimidated. All the guys were wearing their black-and-gold practice gear. And then there was me: I was standing against the wall in my Wake Forest shorts I had bought at the bookstore on my visit the year before.

"Where you get them shorts at, dawg?"

"Oh, I dunno, I think I've had 'em for a while. Someone probably gave 'em to me."

So maybe I was a little paranoid about my image with the guys. Needless to say, the first pickup game ended quickly, and that's when Broderick Hicks pointed at me and asked, "You playin'?"

"Yeah."

"Who you pickin' up?"

"I dunno. Whoever."

"Well, pick somebody, man. We don't got time for this."

This was great: I had to pick four guys from the losing squad to be on my team, which meant I had to tell one guy to sit out. As I looked over my options, I tried to figure out which guy I could afford to not like me, so I chose a freshman, A. W. Hamilton, a point guard from Kentucky, to take a seat. I figured I should get on the upperclassmen's good side.

As I pointed to him, he walked by and glared at me. We were friends, but I don't think we were going to dinner together that night.

The game began, and from the beginning, I remembered the words of Mr. Tuohy: "Don't shoot!" So I passed the ball. Besides, every time I got the ball, I heard my other name: "Little man, I gotcha. Right here, right here, right here. Let me get that. I'll bring it up. Just go to the corner!"

My new teammates obviously didn't know I was already planning on passing every time. My offensive scheme was working beautifully, as my team jumped out to a 5-3 lead. I needed some more tactics on defense, though. I couldn't help but notice what my man would say every time he thought he was open: "Oh, right here, I got this. Gimme the ball. Buddy don't want none!"

Broderick Hicks's face said it all. It was like he was about to take candy from a baby. I knew what my body looked like at the time, so I probably would have been calling for the ball too if I saw a player my size guarding me. This was fine until Broderick started yelling, "Mismatch, mismatch, right here, mismatch!"

I mean, come on, everybody already knew there was a mismatch as soon as I walked into the gym. Did he really have to broadcast it?

These were my thoughts as I attempted to shove Broderick off the block with my hardly robust forearm. "Don't foul me, kid!"

I didn't say anything, but I held my own; and my teammates let me know they were behind me: "Stay in front of him, little man. You got him. I got your help, I got your help!"

That day I used every ounce of strength and quickness God gave me to try and defend those guys. It didn't take me long to discover college basketball was about five times faster than high school. I had never played with guys that were so quick with the ball in the open court. The way they were able to cover ground and get from point A to point B was incredible.

As the other team slowly came back, we were desperate for one more bucket. I hadn't taken a shot the whole game, so naturally my man stopped guarding me, leaving me wide open on the wing. As Craig Dawson penetrated past the right elbow of the free throw line, I passively stood in the corner. My man had left me, and it wasn't hard to see the frustration on Craig's face as he knew he had no choice but to kick me the ball. I caught the pass on a jump stop wide open and quickly glanced at my teammate to the left.

He said, "Swing it, Buddy, swing it."

In the same moment, I looked cross court at the other guard on the weak side: "Skip it, dawg, skip it."

And then I heard Robert O'Kelley's voice: "Knock it down." All in the same second, I squared, jumped, released, and saw the winning shot go through the net. I had hit that shot a thousand times, but the reactions of my teammates made this shot one I'd never forget.

Immediately, Craig approached me with his fist in the air and said, "That's what I'm talking about, little man, bustin' that trey ball. I see you. That's my boy right there." Craig didn't want to pass me the ball to begin with; but now, because I knocked down one jumper, I was suddenly "his boy." I loved it!

I'll Make It.

—JIMMY CHITWOOD, *HOOSIERS*

Needless to say, my team stayed on the court for another game. As soon as I touched the ball, I took a three from NBA range—an air ball. That's when Craig looked at me and said, "Calm down, Buddy, calm down. We'll let you know when you need to shoot again."

7

Suit Up

"Where's Al?"

"He's outside shooting, Mom," my brother yelled.

"Al, it's time to stop playing. No more," Mom insisted.

"I'm coming, Mom. A few more shots."

"Alan, NOW! We're taking our Christmas card picture in twenty minutes, and you've got to shower and change into your nice clothes like your brothers already have."

I kept shooting because I dreaded having to dress up and comb my hair for a picture that wasn't even representative of me. I mean, how many times during the year did I go stand next to a tree with my brothers wearing matching collared blue shirts with sailboats on them? Come on, this wasn't me.

Even at eight years old, I was a *baller*; so why couldn't I just sport my high-tops and hold my ball for the picture? Instead, I knew that I would have to smile and gently hold the hand of my older brother who had probably thrown me on the ground earlier that day. At this point, my name had changed from an affectionate "Al" to "Alan," and then to "Now, Alan Williams!"

"Nuh uh, Dad says you can't stop shooting until you make your last shot. You have to leave on a make." It's not like they were going to take the picture without me.

At this point my mom decided to go to her last resort: "Well, you better make one quick because you have to the count of three to get up stairs: one, two. . . ." I knew never to let my mom's count get to three, so I dropped my ball and ran. Needless to say, in twenty minutes I took a shower, put on my clothes, and was standing by the tree outside.

"All right, here we go," my dad said. "One . . . two . . . three, smile." I felt a little embarrassed that I was wearing the exact same thing as my brothers, but I smiled anyway.

To this day, I often glance at our family photo albums from years past; and when I see my brothers and me standing up against that tree, I can remember how much I disliked having to dress up for those pictures. My dad loved capturing moments on film, and since the days of the sailboat shirts, I too have gained an appreciation for the value of a picture.

In October of my freshman year, everyone involved with the basketball program was at Coach Odom's home celebrating the end of the preseason and the beginning of the regular season. It was a great occasion. There were a number of round tables in Coach's backyard, and all of us indulged in the good food and Southern hospitality. It was an awesome way to cap off the hard work which had taken place that preseason. Coach said, "Thanks for coming guys. We'll see you over at the Joel Coliseum in about thirty minutes to take the team picture."

I was fired up about this picture. I had never been in the

coliseum where we actually played our games. I dreamed of putting on one of those Nike jerseys my whole life, and now I was about to reap the benefits of all my extra hours in the gym. Beyond that, I was excited because I figured that being in the team picture would eliminate the doubts of skeptics who didn't really believe I was on the team.

The locker room was locked when we arrived, so we made our way through a tunnel into the arena. There it was! One of the most beautiful sights I had ever seen! The wood floor glistened, and the Demon Deacon's eye sparkled as I rotated to take in the 14,000 seats staring at me. All of the veteran guys continued their laughing and joking as we walked into the dressing room, where I saw our jerseys hanging in the lockers. I remained silent.

The jerseys didn't have names on them, so I started counting the total number of uniforms with the hope of finding mine. I began to count, but as I turned my body one more time, I couldn't help but notice the two lockers without jerseys. My heart trembled, and I felt my face redden as I heard the guys mumble about something that I didn't even have: "Man, my shorts aren't long enough, dawg." I had gotten over not having an individual shot in the media guide, but I wasn't ready for this. Even one of the players said, "Buddy, that's messed up, man. You gotta be in the picture—you've been out there every day with us."

After the twelve scholarship guys finished changing, I filed out behind them into the arena. The chairs were out; the professional photographer was setting up. Everyone was there, even the secretaries and the team doctor. The only person missing was Coach Odom. I was sitting on the side as everyone began to congregate toward the middle of the floor when one of the assistant coaches walked by me, smirked, and said, "Where's your jersey, Buddy?"

Fifteen minutes later, Coach Odom showed up to an impatient group waiting to get the picture over with. You could even hear a few claps as he walked over to place himself in the middle of the tall players in the back row. As I sat to the side in my khaki pants and short-sleeved collared shirt, I watched the photographer as he began to place various players in different positions.

"All right," he exclaimed, "I need all of your hands behind your back, and I need you guys in front to sit up straight. I wanna make this quick, so work with me."

"Hold up, where's Alan and Matt?" I heard a voice say. Then I heard one of the assistant coaches, "They don't have their jerseys yet, Coach."

Immediately, Coach Odom went over to Sarge. I watched his lips say, "Why don't the walk-ons have jerseys?"

The equipment manager put his hands in the air and said, "I didn't know for sure if they were on the team. Nobody told me otherwise."

Coach Odom responded, "Well, they've been working out with the team for two and a half months! Do we have any extra jerseys around here?" Sarge shrugged his shoulders, and Coach walked back over to his position in the back row. He stood there for a second only to leave again, and headed toward where Matt and I were sitting.

As Coach got closer, he said in a calm voice, "How long would it take you guys to go home, put on a suit and tie and get back here?"

My eyes widened as I said, "About twenty minutes."

As soon as he gave the word, Matt and I took off in a sprint for the door to the sounds of even more groaning players. I was amazed at what Coach Odom had done. Upon arriving at my dorm room, my heart raced as I haphazardly picked out a shirt and tie in my closet. In twenty minutes I went to campus, changed into a coat and tie, and made it back to the arena, where I found myself standing beside one of the scholarship players, picture ready.

"All right, here we go: one ... two ... three."

I was a little embarrassed that I wasn't wearing the same thing as my teammates, but I smiled anyway.

Our job as coaches is to love you.
Your job as players is to love each other.

—JOE EHRMANN

To this day, I often glance at media guides from years past, and when I see my teammates and me standing in that photo, I can remember how much I loved having to dress up for that picture.

My father always says, "Character is the only thing that endures." Through his leadership that night, Coach Odom not only revealed his character, but also showed his willingness to make a decision that most Division One coaches wouldn't have been willing to make. You see, for most coaches, it would have been a *no brainer*: "Sorry we don't have your jersey, Alan. We'll get you in next year's picture."

Everyone knew I wasn't a critical part of our offense, but that night Coach sent a message to the entire program. The message was that the walk-ons were members of the 2000–2001 Wake Forest basketball team, and they were important enough to wait on.

Thanks, Coach.

FIRST HALF
Welcome to the ACC

My freshman year, my gear never seemed to fit. The very first time I put on my uniform I couldn't help but notice how big my warm-up pants were—the XXLs were not made for me.

We always started warm-ups with the tip drill, and as I went up to tip the ball off the backboard, my pants dropped below my knees in front of the whole student section.

You could say that jumping was always a challenge for me, but even more so when I had equipment malfunctions. As a walk-on, I was happy to get a uniform, though, and on the way to the next game, I stopped at the drug store—the safety pins worked like a champ.

8

Tough Transition

I WAS SITTING on the bench seat closest to my high school coach. I was only a sophomore, and with the end of the first quarter approaching, I still hadn't checked into the game. It was one of the first games of the season, and Coach made the decision to start a senior instead of me. Because of the great respect I had for Coach Smith, I didn't complain but played as hard as I could when my name was called.

This particular game was a struggle; and within minutes, we were down to a team we were expected to beat handily. Beyond that, it was a must-win game. With two minutes left in the first quarter, an impatient coach looked down at me, jerked his thumb up in the air, and said, "Get in, Al."

That day our team won the game. I came off the bench and scored 51 points. From that moment on, I was a starter. The next day the Memphis paper read, "Last night, Alan Williams poured in 51 points to break Felix Jones's single game scoring record of 46 points. Williams was 16-20 from the field, 6-8 from 3's, and 13-13 from the free throw line."

Boom! I was on the map. From one single game I gained more attention in my life than I ever had. The local paper listed the top five sophomore players in Memphis, and I was included. There was a brief caption next to each name, and mine stated, "Scored 51 points in a game earlier this year." *USA Today* later named me one of the top twenty players in Tennessee.

I was a shooter. When I warmed up, I could see the opposing team's fans point to me and say—"That's the guy. We gotta stop him." I was a marked man, and during these times in high school basketball, it was as if I had a new label in my life—and I loved it! You would have never known by the way I acted, but in my heart I took great comfort in the fact that I was #12 and that people knew it. Basketball was a big part of my identity.

Almost a thousand days later, I nervously sat in the Wake Forest locker room preparing for my first college practice. It was 5:30 A.M., and I was rummaging through my locker trying to sort through some practice gear. It was a great day for me because I actually had gear! When I put on my shorts, I noticed they were unusually loose.

Now, I knew the style was to wear big shorts, but this was over the top. How could anyone think these shorts fit me! To compensate for my big shorts and my small body, I rolled the elastic band over three times and tucked it into my spandex. As I put on my practice jersey, I noticed I wasn't exactly filling out this part of my uniform either.

I was one of the first to arrive in the locker room that day, so I tightened my shoe laces and went up the stairs into the gym, where I shot alone for nearly ten minutes. As the rest of the guys filed into the gym, I realized—once again—I was not matching my teammates. I had no number on my jersey! All of the other players had numbers on the front and back of their jerseys. I had no time to sulk, though, because Coach Odom had just walked into the gym, which signaled that practice was about to start.

I was tight. This was my very first practice. Never before had I been nervous about making a left-handed lay-up. We started with the three-man weave and immediately I noticed how much faster the drills were going. I had done the weave my whole life; it shouldn't have been difficult for me, but it was. Every time I found myself nearing the beginning of the line, I felt a knot in my stomach that only increased as it got closer and closer for me to go again.

After successfully ending a drill with a lay-up, I went back to the end of the line. One of the older guys subtly pointed out another difference in my practice jersey: "Y'all look at Buddy's WF. It's the one from last year. Buddy didn't even get the new jersey for this year!" That's right, the WF on my jersey was half the size of the letters on the scholarship players' jerseys. Once again, I had no time to think about my "gear inferiority complex" because we had to go to the next drill.

We were in the middle of a two-on-one fast-break sequence. At one point, I was passing back and forth with my teammate as we approached the defender, Josh Howard. Josh was 6'7" and the most wiry and athletic member of our team. The rule of thumb on a fast break was, "Keep attacking the defender until he cuts you off, then pass." As I was in the drill, I knew I was doing everything I was supposed to. I was running the lanes wide, holding the ball in the proper hand, and approaching the basket at the right angle. As I caught the pass on the other side of half court, I began to attack the future NBA star.

I had the ball in my left hand, and as I went at him, my intuition was that Josh assumed there was no way I would have the nerve to try and go by him. On the other hand, I knew that he was certain I would pass if he cut me off. Therefore, I expected him to jab at me and then lunge his body into the passing lane to steal my pass. With this in mind, I kept attacking, and as I approached the free throw line, Josh came at me. I slowed down, looked at the man running with me to my right, quickly put the ball in my right hand to make the pass; and as I did, Josh lunged into the passing lane. A split second later, I stutter-stepped and crossed back over to my left to go in for the lay-up. I knew I had to be quick, so I resorted to a finger roll.

After swiftly guiding the ball up to the left corner of the backboard, I could hear my teammates admiring my move: "No, he didn't; no, he didn't!" As I looked back to make sure the lay-up went through the hoop, I quickly learned my teammates were not *oohing* and *aahing* at my crossing over Josh Howard, but rather at the fact that my nifty finger roll was on top of the air conditioning unit. Apparently, when sizing up the two-on-one situation earlier, I had failed to take into account Josh's recovery time was quicker than most and that there was a possibility he could backhand the ball nearly forty feet in the air—that was the end of the drill.

When Coach huddled up the team, someone said something to the effect of "Welcome to the ACC, Buddy." I felt as if my WF maybe *should* be smaller because all my pride was gone. The rest of the practice was terrible. I dropped passes, forgot plays, and did everything wrong.

The worst feeling in the world was struggling through a drill and hearing one of the coaches say, "Get him out of there!" I tried as hard as I could but still got manhandled. Every time I got the ball, I couldn't think about what I was supposed to be doing because I was too worried about my defender taking the ball away.

After that practice, I dejectedly sat on my stool in a trance. One of my teammates came up and said, "Buddy, you gonna do this next year too?"

With a red face and barely any energy, I looked back at him and said, "Well, yeah."

"Why, dude? You're never gonna play. You didn't even get to play in practice today."

As I took in these hurtful words, I thought for a second, and then said to him, "I'm not giving up."

He smirked and walked off to the showers, leaving me behind in—yet again—one of the low points of that year.

The feelings I felt were far removed from those I had after my fifty-point game in high school. My jersey didn't fit, and my WF

---

*I've come to realize that real growth
of character takes place in the valleys of life.*

—DAVE DRAVECKY

---

was smaller than everyone else's. My identity as a basketball player had taken a 180-degree turn. I had gone from feeling like #12, "the man," to being "no number," the walk-on. My jersey was missing something, and so was my life.

Thinking of these difficult times reminds me of a situation in high school when a reporter interviewed me before my senior year. One of his questions that day caught me off guard. He asked,

"What makes Alan Williams significant?" I replied, "My relationship with the Lord makes me significant." There was no follow up question—that was it. The answer I gave came out naturally, but for some reason, it seemed shallow to throw out such a 'loaded' answer without any sort of explanation. What I'm trying to say is that I'm not sure if I really understood the significance of the word 'significant' in that reporter's question.

In this day and age, it's very common to hear athletes display their faith after scoring the winning touchdown or sinking the buzzer beater. While I would never deny the sincerity of someone thanking God for their gifts on national T.V., I don't think I have ever heard someone from the losing team say those words in an interview. After all, God is still good even in defeat.

Honestly, I can't say that I would recall my faith immediately after a loss, but I do want to be very careful as I tell you my story not to do what I did in that interview in high school and make one line statements to you like, "My faith makes me significant." At least not without telling you *why* and *how* it makes me significant. I tell you this not just because I want you to know, but because I, too, need to make sense of these things and know that I'm not just offering you empty words that sound "spiritual."

Matthew 6:19–20 says, "Do not store up for yourselves treasures on earth…but rather store up for yourselves treasures in heaven.…" I love basketball, but freshman year was a testament to the fact that a sport could not be my ultimate *treasure* because the game constantly let me down. Everything around my basketball experience was continually changing. There were victories and defeats, assists and turnovers, comebacks and lost leads, players healthy and injured, and shooting nights good and bad. It would be hard for me to rationalize putting my faith in something that changed so much, so I'm thankful that God's character is the one thing that remained constant.

I also found in basketball that I always wanted more. I wanted to jump higher, shoot better, and score more. One good game was never enough. While I'm sure elements of this mentality were healthy for sport and maintaining a competitive edge, this trend in my life made me ask the question, "Do I really want to put my faith in fleeting successes?"

Don't get me wrong, making four three-pointers in a row made me very happy. If I were a first round lottery pick in the NBA, that would be incredible. I'm not suggesting success is a bad thing. But none of my successes to this point have brought me

---

For where your treasure is, there your heart will be also.

—MATTHEW 6:21

---

lasting fulfillment. It seems like it would be sad to get to the end of life only to look back and realize that I've just searched for one temporary success after another.

J.I. Packer gave me perspective on earthly joy and success when he suggested that "The best things in life are merely *signposts* pointing to something much greater."

I've tried to find identity in being on the Wake Forest basketball team, trying to get the right job out of college, and even through writing this book. I've tried to find that one thing. I've searched and searched, but in the end I always come to the same conclusion: the same conclusion that another man came to after sitting on the bench—except he won 10 national titles while coaching UCLA:

I always tried to make clear that basketball was not the ulti-mate. It is of small importance in comparison to the total life we live. There is only one kind of life that truly wins, and that is the one that places faith in the hands of the Savior. Until that is done, we are on an aimless course that runs in circles and goes nowhere (John Wooden).

Those words, of course, from a man who accomplished what every coach dreams of. So, I'm not sure what I would have said if the media had interviewed me after that terrible first practice. But today, I can reflect on dismal points in my freshman year and be thankful. I am thankful that there was a time in my life when I found myself without a number because those days enabled me to understand that the most important label of my life could not be found on a jersey.

9

More than a Moment

I LOVED preparation. While I was growing up, my dad taught me the importance of preparing for each moment. He always knew famous quotes and sayings which reminded me that preparation and routine were vital to an aspiring athlete. In fact, I felt the routine I followed before a game was, in many ways, what set me apart from other athletes I played against in high school. Whether it was my free-throw routine—three dribbles and a deep breath—or the things I did between the end of the last school bell and game time, I was consistent.

When I was a kid I watched Michael Jordan and Larry Bird videos and saw how meticulous they were in their preparation. Like every kid, I wanted to be just like them, so I created my own routine that I followed before every game. After school, I would shoot around at a nearby church, come home, and eat a steak while watching the last twenty minutes of *Hoosiers*.

In addition, my dad consistently went into my room and laid my uniform out on my bed. It was a tradition. He left me a new sweatband for every game (I always wore one on the left wrist). I had to have my wristband. One game I forgot it, and can remember walking out to center circle for tip-off and raising my left hand at my dad, shrugging my shoulders. I was flustered, but before I knew it, I could see my little brother Bo charging down from the stands with something in his hand. That day I learned my dad always carried an extra sweatband in his pocket—that's preparation!

Before each game, my dad would also give me an index card with a Bible verse and a little advice to encourage me. These were the things that, to this day, serve as some of my happiest memories in basketball.

- NO CHEAP FOULS
- BE MENTALLY TOUGH
- BLOCK OUT
- INSPIRE YOUR TEAMMATES AND COACHES WITH YOUR WORK ETHIC
- HAVE FUN AND PLAY TO WIN
* SUCCESS IS WHERE PREPARATION MEETS OPPORTUNITY

PROVERBS 16:3
COMMIT TO THE LORD WHATEVER YOU DO, AND YOUR PLANS WILL SUCCEED.

Though my routine may seem excessive, I can honestly say that in high school I always felt like the most mentally prepared player on the court.

While this approach was important to me in high school, I was forced to deviate from it in college. There, the coaches determined much of our preparation; it was about the whole team. A Saturday game routine looked like this one:

A.M.
10:00: Shoot around in practice uniforms
11:30: Rest

P.M.
3:00:   Walk-thru—go over all the other team's plays (the scout team and I ran their plays)
3:30:   Pregame meal (Ryan's Steak and Chophouse)
5:05:   Leave for arena
5:15:   Shoot around on own in arena
6:00:   Team meeting
6:15:   Full team stretch
6:30:   Team warm-up
6:50:   Five-minute meeting; Lord's Prayer
6:56:   Last-minute warm-ups
7:00:   Introductions, *Star-Spangled Banner*
7:05:   Tip-off
7:06:   Take my seat at end of bench

I can still feel the anxiety I had as I prepared for my first college game. I was nervous about everything—from missing a lay-up in warm-ups to looking awkward as we bounced around in the huddle at center court.

While this was only an exhibition game, it was still the first time the city of Winston-Salem would come to Joel Coliseum to see us play. We were playing the Nike Elite All-Stars, a number of former college players trying to make it to the pro level. After our walk-thru, we ate our pregame meal, and then I met my parents who had driven from Memphis for the big occasion. I gave each of my parents a letter in which I told them I loved them and how much it meant to me that they were there to share with me a life-long dream.

Upon arriving at the arena for my very first game, I felt like a *big-timer.* As I saw all the fans filing into the arena from the main doors, I swiftly maneuvered my car down a side street and pulled into the back entrance of the coliseum. After pulling up to the gate, the security guard with the yellow jacket squinted his eyes to see who I was. That's when I pointed at the pink sticker on my mirror. *That's right—I'm supposed to be here,* I thought to myself.

The locker room was a sight to see. One of the best feelings I've ever had was walking into that dressing room and finally seeing my equipment laid out perfectly in my locker. It was really there. I still remember seeing my jersey for the first time: I was #20. Someone once asked how I chose my number. I told them I showed up for the first game and that's what they gave me. Number 20 . . . sounds good, I'll take it. In reality, it could have been any number, and I still would have liked it. I just wanted that jersey!

After putting on my equipment, I walked through the tunnel and shot around to the rap music playing inside the arena. You would have thought I was a starter by the number of shots I took out there. Thirty minutes later, we began to stretch, and then, huddled up to say the Lord's Prayer. At the conclusion of the prayer, we began to jump up and down, shoving each other around in the huddle.

I don't think it was until my senior year that I really figured out how to get properly pumped up in the huddle. That night, it was like most of my dancing experiences. You have to get comfortable first and then you can begin to do your thing. Next came my favorite part of all as I heard the words through the tunnel into the arena, "Leeeet's get ready to ruuuumble!" The loud pump-up music followed, and I began to file out with the cheerleaders and my teammates for the very first time.

Thankfully, I made all of my lay-ups in warm ups, and each time I ran back to the end of the line, I smiled at my parents who were waving in the stands. Twenty minutes later, the warm-ups ended, and that's when the lights went off for introductions. As the spotlight shined on our huddle, it hit me. I had made it! There was something about those lights going off that was surreal enough to make me put what I had done in perspective.

With nearly five minutes to go in the fourth quarter, we were up almost twenty points and I began to hear a few of the students and fans yelling, "Put in the walk-ons, Coach; Put in number twenty." I was sure I was the only one hearing those words, but moments later I heard a group of about fifteen guys chanting as loud as they could, "We want Alan—*clap, clap*—we want Alan." You could barely hear these sounds in the 14,000-seat arena. Moments later, other members of the student section began to catch on; and within another twenty seconds, the whole student body simultaneously chanted, "We want Alan—*clap, clap*—we want Alan."

As I sat in my seat, I didn't know what to do. I began to get that knot in my stomach I had become accustomed to. I chose to play it cool, though, and concealed my emotion. My teammates began to nudge me and pull at my arm. I saw the annoyance on the assistant coaches' faces. Despite their disapproval, it began to get louder and louder in those next two minutes. It wasn't my fault. I didn't know *all* of these people. I couldn't do anything about it.

It was apparent that the students wanted me in the game. I figured they liked me because they could relate to me. We watched the game the same way—sitting down. And beyond that, they probably thought, "If that guy can be out there, so can I." The chant directly behind our bench grew louder, and finally Coach Odom walked down to my end of the bench. The chant got even louder. He put two of his fingers in the air and said, "You two, now." At that moment, everybody in the building went wild. As soon as he gave the word, I jumped out of my seat, took off my warm-up, and ran to the scorer's table with Matt.

I was now waiting for my big moment—the first time ever in a college game. The horn blew and then I heard, "Now checking into the game, number twenty, Alan Williams." Again, the fans went crazy as I slapped Ervin's hand to find out who I was guarding. We were about to inbound the ball at half court. At this point, my mind was so scattered I couldn't remember the offense. I think I just ran to the corner to spot up; that's usually what I did when I didn't know what to do (I was always given a hard time for that.).

The first play, A.W. dribbled the ball up the floor and swung it to the left side of the court. As the ball was swung back to him at the top of the key, I thought, *I think I'm about to get the ball here.* The ball came my direction. I caught it immediately, and that's when the ex-Alabama star rushed out at me. I did everything you're not supposed to do—I took two dribbles away from the basket and picked up my dribble.

My defender swarmed me, stuck his hand in my shooting pocket, and ripped the ball out of my hands. He took off with the ball for the other end as I raced to cut him off. It was a two-on-one break, and I was the *one.* As I saw him make the pass to his teammate, I noticed it was unusually high, so I jumped; and as I jumped, I bumped the player trying to score. The bump, however, wasn't enough to avoid getting dunked on: I mean, really dunked on—like "take a picture and put it on a poster" bad.

It was nasty. It was the worst possible scenario. I got stripped, alley-ooped on, and to top it off, I fouled the guy. It was everything that you didn't want to happen when you went into the game. I could feel the vibrations of the arena at this point. It was as if everybody was saying, "Whoa, that was rough. I feel bad for that guy."

There were only seventeen seconds left in the game. I had already run up the left side of the floor. The ball was in-bounded on the baseline, and before I knew it, the ball was coming to me on a baseball pass up the sideline. I was standing near the coaches' box at the time, and as soon as I caught the ball, it was as if the entire arena yelled at the same time, "Shoooooot." The same player who stripped me earlier was closing out on me, and as he lunged at me to contest, I followed the arena's command and let a bomb go from nearly twenty-six feet.

When I released the shot, I couldn't see the ball in the air because my defender blocked my view. As he cleared past me, I saw a ball go through a net to the loudest roar of the night! The place went nuts, my teammates went crazy; and immediately Rafael Vidaurreta came up and hugged me as the time on the clock expired: "Yeah, Buddy. Way to go, Buddy."

Immediately, I looked at my mom and dad who were not far off in the stands. My mom was clearly in tears. She had seen me score since I was six years old, but for some reason, this basket was special. Maybe I could understand why she was emotional: she loved me. No one had prayed for me more that fall than my mom, and only she knew how difficult the journey had been.

The next day was the homecoming football game, and as I walked my date to the tailgate party, many of the fraternity guys began to clap for me. You see, this was the group of guys that had started the chant; and as they came up to shake my hand, they said things like, "Alan, you're the man. You realize what you did last night? You scored in a Wake Forest basketball game."

I humbly accepted the compliment because I knew that, in reality, they had no idea. They knew that I made a three-pointer,

---

Confidence is the result of hours and days and weeks
and years of constant work and dedication.

—ROGER STAUBACH

---

but they had no idea what that preseason had been like: the push-ups, the travel bag, or the team picture. They had no idea how many nights I went to that gym to practice with Rob nor how many hours I spent preparing to make a shot like that. For those guys and the rest of the fans watching, it was about a moment in time—two minutes on the court. For me, the ball going through the net that night was about the twelve years of hard work that took place before I ever released that shot. It was about the basketball camps, the drills, the conditioning, and all the nights I spent shooting in my backyard as a kid. I didn't think so much about the moment; I thought about the ways in which I prepared for that moment.

While my first game reminded me my role from high school to college had changed, some things remained the same. Hours before my first game at Wake, I opened an envelope. My dad had not forgotten. In the envelope was an index card with two things written in black ink: Proverbs 16:3, which says, "Commit your work to the Lord and your plans will succeed"; and at the bottom was the quote my dad had reminded me of since I was a little kid, "Success is where preparation meets opportunity."

In that first game of my college career, an opportunity came, and although it was only a small one—I was ready.

10

Harassment on the Road

"HEY Y'ALL, look, it's Opie. Little Opie. Look how cute he is."

"Yeah, it is. Hey Opie, yeah you . . . Aunt Bee been baking you some apple pies lately?"

"You better make your shots or I'm going to tell the sheriff."

This was my welcome to the University of Virginia. As I walked into the gym for the shoot-around before the game, one of the 800-plus students surrounding the court pointed out that I resembled the character Opie on *The Andy Griffith Show*—I was heckled from that point on. Fans on the road in the ACC were brutal, and after that experience, I was determined to find a way to escape the harassment of the opposing team's fans during shoot-arounds before games.

Days after my memorable trip to Charlottesville, our chartered plane flew into Baltimore. We were playing Maryland. This particular game, I decided that, in order to avoid being picked on, I would walk in for the shoot-around with one of our best players, Darius Songaila, a powerful 6'9" Lithuanian. I figured the fans would associate me with a good player and give me some respect, not scrutinizing my every step.

As we arrived in the locker room at Cole Field House that night, Matt (the other walk-on) quickly took off his warm-ups and proceeded into the arena, but I was determined to carry out my plan. I had to be subtle; I didn't want Darius to know I had been scheming. I was getting nervous though, as I could hear the *boos* my other teammates received as they walked into the arena. I persisted with my plan, tying and untying my shoes three times. Finally, Darius got up from his chair.

As I followed Darius down the open corridor, I could see thousands of students on each side of the court waiting for prime heckling material like myself. My heart was pounding, and as Darius was about to enter the tunnel into the gym, I quickened my pace to catch up, now directly behind him. Seconds later, our initial walk into the arena was over. I could hear nothing—that is, until we went to get balls off the rack to shoot.

It was at this point someone yelled, "Darius Songaila, you're an illegal alien. You're not allowed in Maryland." I was behind Darius, and as I grabbed my ball, I couldn't help but smirk at the originality of their remarks. Fans always used to give Darius a hard time for being a foreigner. As I chuckled at the cleverness of the fan's comments, the same voice yelled from the stands, "And nobody said you could bring your twelve-year-old little brother in here either!" Once again, my attempts to avoid harassment had failed.

One Saturday afternoon, our team traveled to Cameron Indoor Stadium at Duke University. I knew if I couldn't hold off being the joke at UVA and Maryland, my chances of surviving the "Cameron Crazies" were slim. I had watched their antics on national TV for most of my life, and now I was going directly into their presence. I had no plan at this point. Throughout that week, the fans had been camping in what they call "Krzyzewskiville." They were eager. They were like hostile lions ready to be let out of their den.

As we all began to file off the bus, I could see the students waiting to get into the arena on the other side of the small gymnasium. Their chants began before we even entered the arena: "This is our house—*clap clap*—this is our house!"

I couldn't believe I was actually about to dress out for a game in Cameron. I had shot there as a kid once, and now I was a player. It was difficult to be this nostalgic as I warmed up with all the commotion around me. Students were yelling, and as always, Dick Vitale was pacing about the arena. There was a lot going on—I saw things that day I had never seen before.

Robert O'Kelley, our marquee player at the time, was in a shooting slump. As I glanced at the student section adjacent to the court, I noticed a student holding a giant milk carton. I'm not sure how it got there, but a picture of Robert from junior high was blown up on the back of that carton. Underneath the classic photo of Rob were big black letters that said MISSING, along with his recent shooting stats.

Right then and there, I figured out why Duke fans were rumored to be so tough. They spent just as much time plotting for basketball games as they did studying for classes. They even had copies of our team's media guide floating around the stands.

As I continued to warm up, I couldn't believe I had not been targeted yet. With a few road trips already under my belt, I wasn't too worried about it. Every player got picked on. Who cares, right?

Those thoughts came easy then, but when one of my shots

bricked off the side of the rim and bounced directly into the student section, I did care. So there I was, at the Crazies' mercy—I would have never gone after that ball had I known it was going to bounce over the rail.

I stood in front of the student section and coolly stuck my hand out to get the ball from the obnoxious guy in the front row. While waiting for the fan to hand the ball back, they began the traditional "Water boy...you'll never play...you must love benches." I had heard it all, but as the guy launched the ball over my head toward the direction of the back board, one student said something I will never forget: "Hey twenty, you're the man. You gotta love a guy who is just out here for the love of the game."

By now, I had the ball back in my hands, and as the student said these words, everyone began to laugh hysterically. I digested their sarcasm for a couple of seconds, took one dribble toward the basket, turned 180 degrees back toward the students, and chucked the Wilson ball in the guy's face. Of course, I didn't do that, but I wanted to.

That day, in Durham, North Carolina, I knew I wasn't going to get any playing time or score any points. I was going to sit on the end of the bench and encourage my teammates as much as I possibly could. Why? Because that was my role—and yes, I do love the game.

HALF-TIME
Don't Give Up

Practices were my games, but when it came to the real games, I knew not to look at the coach unless we were up by a sizable margin. During my freshman year, we were up at least twenty-five points on the University of Virginia at home, so, with good reason, I began to look down the bench at Coach Odom.

After a little pressure from the crowd, Coach walked down toward my end and signaled with his hand that it was time for me to go in. So all in one motion, I got up, took off my warm-ups, and sprinted to the scorer's table. I was ready...or was I?

As I took a knee to wait for the next dead ball, Coach Odom signaled me back to the bench. I walked back over to him; and as I got close enough, he put his arm around me, looked me in the eye, and said, "Alan, who are you going in for?" I thought for a second and then looked back at him with an honest face: "I dunno, Coach." Coach smiled back at me: "It always helps to know that, doesn't it?"

11

Three Minutes

IT WAS the week of the first round of the NCAA Tournament. The selection show on CBS two days before revealed we would be playing Butler, a mid-major school from Indiana. The game would be played in Kansas City, Missouri.

Despite making it to postseason play, the morale of our team was low. It was tournament time, and we weren't clicking as a unit. Coach's frustration was reflected in his threats to the team in practice: "Don't test me. Don't any of you test me. Go ahead, some of you just keep going like you are. Bring that attitude up to Kansas City, and I promise I won't play any of you. I'll put Alan Williams in the game if I have to. Just wait."

First of all, I personally didn't know whether to take these comments as an encouragement or as an insult. I suppose on the one hand it was nice to have my name mentioned in a reference to actually getting to play, but it wasn't all that flattering to be portrayed as the last resort either.

Seriously, though, our team was in trouble. We started out the year with a 12–0 record, climbing in the rankings to #3 in the country. To begin ACC play that month, we squared off against the also nationally ranked North Carolina Tar Heels. We were in control most of the game, but as the final seconds ticked away on the clock, UNC got a tip-in to beat us at the buzzer. It was a demoralizing defeat. As we continued into conference play, it was as if we never fully recovered, never showing any signs of consistency.

Despite the slippage, it was still a memorable regular season, especially getting to travel to all of the different schools in the ACC. I couldn't help but be wide-eyed as I walked into all the different arenas. Every game was a challenge in our conference. There were no cupcakes. And winning home games was a must. Beyond FSU and Clemson, any road win was a bonus that year.

My playing time was minimal to quite minimal that regular season. The blowout wins I was accustomed to seeing before Christmas were now close games that almost always went down to the wire. Whenever the opportunity presented itself, however, Coach Odom made sure the walk-ons played. I played thirty seconds against Virginia at home and was fortunate to hit a last-second scoop shot over their starting point guard, Donald Hand, to help secure a twenty-seven-point lead. I like to think of all my "made" shots in college as last-second shots. It just sounds better.

I also received an opportunity to play against Clemson on the road. I decided to show the crowd at Littlejohn Coliseum that night what a running hook shot from six feet looked like. The crowd was truly dazzled even though it hit the back of the rim. My dad was there, and he definitely appreciated my innovation. As a walk-on, I had to be crafty, you know—scoops, hooks, whatever it took.

Even though our team ended up finishing the ACC regular season around .500, we still finished fourth in the conference. Everybody gets beat up in our league. Going into the ACC Tournament, I could sense that our chemistry was gone. The locker room was not exactly an uplifting environment, and players were getting frustrated with one another on the court. From my angle, I sensed jealousy between the different recruiting classes, a problem that was capable of hindering our team's progress even more than bad spacing on offense.

In early March, we traveled to Atlanta to the site of the 2001 ACC Tournament in hopes that we could recapture the glory days of 1995 and 1996. From the outset, the atmosphere seemed like a Final Four I had attended one time in high school. It was incredible, one of the biggest events of the year, and I'll never forget the hype that surrounded that entire week. I felt pretty important as I rode the bus to the Georgia Dome, escorted by a motorcade through every intersection.

I remember exactly what it felt like being in the tunnel with my teammates as we waited our turn to run out. Duke's game ended, and before I knew it, Mike Dunleavy, Jason Williams, Carlos Boozer, Chris Duhon, and Coach Krzyzewski passed by my left shoulder. Like my other teammates in front of me, I gave a little head nod to a few of their players, but didn't get a lot of feedback in return. The butterflies that invaded my stomach as we huddled up one more time were overwhelming; and as we trotted along the blue carpet near the court, I made sure not to trip over the camera cords running along the ground.

As we made our way out of the tunnel, I looked up to see the 34,000 screaming fans. To this point, I had warmed up in a number of arenas, but never before had I experienced anything like this. As I dribbled in for my first lay-up, I wondered how many of those fans were looking at our basket. After I made it, I saw one of my friends from high school waving at me with his dad in the distance. Seeing my buddy Matt reminded me how incredibly far I had come. The largest crowd I ever saw in high school was maybe two thousand people, but now I was going through lay-up lines on the biggest stage of all.

That night, we faced off against the Maryland Terrapins which meant that we would be heavily challenged at every position. Juan Dixon and Steve Blake gave us all we could handle in the backcourt, and Lonnie Baxter was no slouch in the post. In addition, one of our players, Craig Dawson, separated his shoulder in the first half. Nothing was going our way that game, and the score in the end reflected it.

As I shook Coach Gary Williams's unusually sweaty hand, I trotted back into the tunnel where one of our players, Josh Howard, was yelling at one of the Maryland players. Josh claimed that for the entire game Byron Mouton had been grabbing his backside on purpose. Josh, rightly so, did not take a liking to it.

Eventually, we pulled Josh away and steered him in the direction of our locker room where he was assured to be touched by no one. With an injured Craig Dawson in another room with G.C., our trainer, we all sat in the locker room and waited the arrival of a disappointed coach.

Despite our bad showing in Atlanta, Coach assured us that we should keep our heads up, because in forty-eight hours, for the first time in four years, Wake would be announced as one of the final sixty-five teams in the country.

After finding out we would be playing Butler, surprisingly we began two-a-day practices. Since it was spring break, Coach had the luxury of doing this sort of thing. As tension continued to mount on our team, players became less coachable and coaches more irritable. Now we were back to where we started: Coach Odom was threatening our players with the idea of putting me in the game.

Days later, we flew into Kansas City with what we thought was a great number seven seed. Butler was a solid team. But as I watched them warm up at the other end of the court, I saw their size and immediately thought, *if we play our cards right—I could get some action tonight.* This was not the case, however, as Butler ran out of the gate with a most embarrassing lead.

"We couldn't hit anything, and they were hitting everything" was the best way to sum up what was happening. With ten minutes to go in the first half, we had maybe scored ten points. Even worse, we were down by thirty by the end of the half. It was embarrassing, and at half time, one of the assistant coaches made it clear just how embarrassing it was. Frank Haith (now head coach for Miami), normally a mild-mannered guy, slammed his hand down on the table and said in a few more descriptive words, "You guys are better than this. It's time to get it in gear!"

Although our locker room was full of players that day, it was really quite empty. For whatever reason, the motivation was not there, and the second half diminished any chances of chipping away at the large lead.

After the game, I felt for the seniors who were crying at their respective lockers. Their college careers were over. I could not help but cringe as I watched Robert O'Kelley, the player who had been so instrumental in my life that year, now taking his jersey off for the very last time. I watched carefully as Dan Collins, a writer from the *Winston-Salem Journal,* shook O'Kelley's hand, telling him how much he admired what he had done in his career and how he respected the way he had represented the university.

The day after our loss, I got on the elevator, where I stood alone with Coach Odom and his wife. We didn't say much, but as we gradually made it down to the lobby, I was reminded how much pressure college coaches have on them.

Being a basketball coach at a high-profile school like Wake Forest was, in my opinion, one of the best and worst jobs. The fans loved Coach when the team was doing well, but clearly questioned him when we were struggling. Odom had won back-to-back ACC Championships and made multiple appearances in the NCAA Tournament. He was a great coach, and as his book said, he knew that *The End Is Not the Trophy.* There was more to the two-time ACC Coach of the Year. Coach was a Christian; he had a lovely wife, two sons who followed him into the coaching profession, and a black lab, Brooks.

I liked Coach Odom. He was always the same to me. In the midst of critical threads on message boards and negative articles written by columnists during this time, I could not help but sympathize with the life of a coach—a profession where it seems like you're only as good as your last game.

A few weeks after our season ended, I finally adjusted to my new schedule without practice every day. I filled my time with my favorite hobby, golf, and paid closer attention to the friendships I was forced to abandon for much of the regular season. One day I found myself walking on the lower quad of our campus talking on my cell phone with my best friend on the team, Steve Lepore, a transfer from Northwestern. I was trying to figure out when our tee time was that day, when he suddenly cut me off and told me that we'd better hustle to the athletic center for weightlifting because we were late.

Wait a minute, I thought. *Nobody ever told me anything about weights.* I hadn't received an e-mail or a phone call; nobody told me workouts were starting back up again. I assumed it was a mistake

---

Sports do not build character . . . they reveal it.

—JOHN WOODEN

---

and ran to my dorm to change into my practice shorts. Soon after, with my heart racing, I hustled over to the athletic center, opened the door to the weight room and walked in. Thankfully, I wasn't late just yet, but the whole team was already sitting down waiting to hear instructions from our strength coach.

Just as I sat down to join the rest of the guys in the corner of the room, I looked to my left and saw the door to the weight room swing open. It was Coach Sanderson. Our eyes happened to meet, and as they did, he motioned me over toward the door. I trotted over and he said, "Come to my office right quick, Buddy." I knew I was going to miss the first part of weights, but I had no choice but to follow him up the stairs.

At this point the knot in my stomach was as big as ever, and the staircase seemed endless. What was about to happen to me? Coach Sanderson had also gotten in touch with Matt, the other walk-on, and together we walked into our assistant coach's office. "Shut that door behind you, guys," Coach said as he stood beside his desk. "Guys, the reason I had y'all come in here is because I feel like I need to be honest with you fellas. We as a staff are not going to be able to guarantee that you guys will have a position on next year's team. Don't get me wrong, you guys did a great job this year; it's not because of anything you did or didn't do. Quite frankly, we don't even know if we're going to have a walk-on next year—we just have so many guards right now. You guys are certainly welcome to come back next year to tryouts if we have them, but right now, in fairness to you all, we're just going to focus on the scholarship guys and not have any walk-ons work out with the team. I'm sorry to have to be the bad guy. We'll see y'all around, I'm sure."

I could feel my face getting red. I couldn't say anything as I walked down the stairs with Matt. Each step felt like I was walking deeper and deeper into a hole—my legs felt heavy.

The car remained quiet as Matt and I drove away from the athletic center. Matt said, "I guess we're done. I wanna transfer anyway, especially if that's the way they're going to be. I don't really care."

After Matt got out of the car, I drove down a side street and pulled into a parking lot behind my dorm. I sat there for a few minutes and thought about what had just happened. I was distraught. Where had I gone wrong? How could they do this to me? I put so much into that season! Sure, I struggled along the way, but I gave everything I had! Coach had told me that I could play for four years. Why was I now being told otherwise?

By this time, I had picked up my cell phone to call home. As soon as I heard my mom's voice, I lost it. I cried. I hadn't cried in probably five years, but that day tears flowed from my eyes. I cried because something that I loved was leaving me.

That Wednesday in April of my freshman year, I learned that in life, our positions are never guaranteed. For the first time in twelve years, my life was without basketball. I had walked into a coach's office, and three minutes later it was gone.

12

Coach?

"ALAN, you know you belong on that team. You just gotta make up your mind that you're going to find a way to get back on."

My brother Campbell was right. Soon after visiting him and his friends at Furman University, I was determined to find a way to get my jersey back. While my meeting with Coach Sanderson five days before was certainly not promising, it wasn't going to be enough to make me go away. Next year's season was a long way off; and I knew that, in order to get back on the team, I had to be relentless in my pursuit.

During the three-hour drive back to Winston-Salem, I prayed about my situation. I knew that getting on the team was not going to happen overnight; therefore, being patient was going to be a necessary virtue—a virtue that I didn't have on my own.

In the months after being cut, my mom encouraged me to trust in the "still perfect" plans that the Lord had for me and cautioned that it was too overwhelming to look too far down the road. The only way I would enjoy the pursuits of my life would be to take them one step at a time, an undertaking that was so much easier said than done.

One of the first steps in getting my jersey back was to go talk to the people that were willing to help me. I dropped by the weight

---

Ability is what you're capable of doing.
Motivation determines what you do.
Attitude determines how well you do it.

—LOU HOLTZ

---

room the Monday I got back from South Carolina and informed the strength coach that I was no longer allowed to work out with the team. In spite of these things, I asked if he would still be willing to work with me in the weight room on an individual basis. I needed some power to my game, and thankfully, he had no problem with me being around. He told me, "If you wanna get better, Buddy, I'll help you."

So I began to come in at odd times during the day to do just that. The week after being cut, I showed up everyday. It was hard to be away from my teammates. I hated running into them because it reminded me of what had happened. Honestly, I think they hated it, too. Each of them knew how badly I wanted to be on that team. I remember the emptiness I felt as I lifted at one end of the weight room while, together, they lifted at the opposite end. I may have gotten close to them during these times, but in my heart, they felt far away.

I can also vividly remember what it was like to see Coach

Odom's face when he saw that I was still working out. I could see the surprise in his eyes as if to say, "You're gonna keep on coming, huh?"

That's right, I was going to keep on coming; and it just so happened that everywhere I went, I happened to run into Coach. In addition to lifting more, I had also decided to run three miles each morning. As I passed the athletic center around 7:00 A.M. one day, I saw Coach Odom again, who happened to be strolling by. Naturally I picked up my pace even more and said to him, "Mornin', Coach." I didn't stop to talk; but as I ran, I heard him mutter, "Wow," as only Coach could do. During those few weeks, I wanted to show Coach that it was going to take a lot more than a meeting with his assistant coach to keep me away from the game I loved.

On April 10, 2001, my tactic of sending a message to Coach Odom became meaningless. I was walking on the upper quad area of campus and happened to run into Broderick Hicks, our junior point guard from Houston, Texas. I had just finished running on my own again, and as I gasped for a few breaths of air, he walked past me and said, "Hey, Buddy, we got weights today at four. Be there."

"Wait a minute," I said, "you know I'm not allowed to work out with you guys. Coach said I couldn't be there, remember?"

"Coach Odom isn't the coach anymore, Buddy. We just had a meeting. He resigned. He's goin' to South Carolina." Confusedly, I looked back at him for a second and tried to figure out what he was saying. "Wake up, Buddy. I'm the coach now, and I say you're coming to weights at four P.M." With a shocked look on my face, I watched Broderick as he walked off. I said in a calm voice, "I'll be there."

I took off in a sprint. As I passed the athletic center, I could see five news trucks already getting the scoop; players were being interviewed. It was like there was a weird buzz going around

---

In his heart a man plans his course,
but the Lord determines his steps.

—PROVERBS 16:9

---

campus—the man who had given me my start at Wake Forest was now gone. For the first time in thirteen years, Wake was going to have a new coach. On this day, however, Broderick claimed he was the coach, and so I went straight to my dorm, changed, and hustled back to the weight room for the first time in three weeks.

I had mixed emotions at the thought of Coach Odom leaving, but didn't have time to think about it as I raced across the campus. I just couldn't get over how good it felt to have the captain of the team want me back. Arriving in the weight room that day, I saw all of my teammates. That's when they smiled and said, "Buddy's back!"

As we lined up for our step-ladder drills, a series of agility exercises, I couldn't help but notice all of the new off-season gear that the guys had already been given. All of them were wearing matching gray t-shirts and black shorts. I, of course, didn't have any of that stuff; my shorts and t-shirt were not anything like theirs, but for the first time, I didn't care. I didn't care because in the three weeks I was away from them, I wasn't concerned about dressing *like* my teammates; I just wanted to be *with* them. I wanted to sweat with them. I wanted to laugh with them. And I wanted to struggle with them. I wanted back on that team!

So as my turn came to do the drill, I looked down at the fifteen-foot rope ladder on the floor, took a deep breath, and began to chop my feet. I made sure I took the ladder one step at a time, because I knew that if I didn't, I wouldn't make it through the drill. Working out that day was the beginning of trying to get my name back on the roster. To be honest, I didn't know exactly how it was going to happen, but I was determined to take whatever steps necessary in order to keep my basketball dreams alive.

13

Everywhere

"AT EIGHT tonight, I need all you guys to show up in the Rovere Room. Supposedly a candidate for the new coaching job is coming in town tonight. Don't be late. Oh, and this is only for the scholarship guys." These words came from an employee in the athletic department. The field of coaches had obviously been narrowed, and we were about to see the results from the search—with the exception of me, since I wasn't a scholarship player. As soon as these instructions were given, a few of the players leaned over to me and said, "Buddy, you're coming; don't worry about that."

To be honest, I was a little nervous about going to the meeting without an invitation, but I figured the players' wanting me to be there was enough. It was like going to a wedding when you're not invited. Nobody does that sort of thing, but I was about to do it anyway. Besides, I had come too far to be passive now.

Later that afternoon, while watching TV, I heard Skip Prosser of Xavier was flying into Winston-Salem on a private plane to finalize his contract with Wake Forest officials and meet with members of his new team. That included me. I was a member, or at least posing as one.

Illegitimately, I showed up for the meeting that night and took my seat in the second row of chairs lined up on the right side of the room. Five minutes later, Coach Prosser walked in with his assistants, Coach Gaudio and Coach Mack. I remember everything: Coach Prosser was wearing a green shirt, khakis, and a couple of extra pounds he would later work off. Before any words were spoken, the new coach came around and individually shook each of our hands. He looked me straight in the eye, squeezed my hand, and introduced himself, "Skip Prosser."

"Alan Williams," I said as I squeezed extra hard just like my dad taught me. As he greeted me, I was almost certain he thought I was the manager. I suppose I'll never know, but as the meeting began, I took in every detail. I knew that adapting to the new staff's ways was the only hope of getting my jersey back.

Soon after, Ron Wellman, our athletic director, formally introduced Coach Prosser as our new basketball coach. He reminded us that this particular coach was one of the best in the country and how privileged we were to have him. Moments later, Coach Prosser was given command, and after talking for just a few short moments, I learned these coaches were all business. Coach outlined his expectations for us as student-athletes by saying that our code while we were here was as simple as ABC:

Academics
Basketball
Conduct

These were to be the three important aspects of our lives at Wake Forest, and if we were unable to perform in these three areas, then we were not cut out for the type of program he would be running. I also saw this serious nature played out when the new coach caught a player in the front row off guard, and stopped the conversation to say, "Hey, I need you to look me in the eye when I'm talking to you. I wanna see your eyes."

Not only was I staring at Coach, I wasn't blinking. Especially later, when Coach Gaudio said, "I'm telling you fellas. You better get in shape, 'cause this conditioning in the fall"—and then he paused—"it's not gonna be fun."

Everything about the meeting that night was intentional. Toward the end, we signed up for individual workouts which would be held the next day. Coach said, "We can't afford to waste anytime. Let's get right into it tomorrow." This was most impressive to me: he was not going to be publicly introduced as our new head coach until the following afternoon, yet individual workouts were already being scheduled. Once again, I admired the new sense of urgency evident in this coaching staff. As I walked to my dorm room after the long meeting, I became nervous about performing in the workouts the following day.

So, there I was—having already been cut once—with a new beginning. I still wondered if Coach had discovered what had happened three weeks before his arrival, but now was not the time to worry. I would continue to show up for workouts just as I had the previous two weeks.

During this process, it was also apparent that Matt, the other walk-on, had decided to stop playing. He hadn't been around since our meeting with Coach Sanderson and didn't show up for the team meeting that night. I had a great deal of respect for the fact that Matt endured the same challenges I had as a walk-on our freshman year. He was tough, and in many ways, had handled the physical aspect of being a walk-on much better than I had.

I'll never forget all the nights we went to Krispy Kreme and encouraged each other through our struggles. To this day, only Matt could identify with anything that happened to me that freshman year. He was there every step of the way, and now, his desires had taken him in another direction. Matt continued to pursue the possibilities of transferring to UNC in preparation for a career in medicine, and I missed him.

As for me, I was still around. The door wasn't open, but it wasn't closed either. It was cracked, and I knew the next day I would begin my attempts to knock at Coach Prosser's door with the hope he might let me in.

Ironically, the next day it wasn't me that did the knocking. I showed up for my three o'clock workout ten minutes early, and as I dribbled my ball to the other end of the court, I heard a voice: "Alan, come here for a second."

I was surprised to hear my name. I was used to being called Buddy, and beyond that, I couldn't believe that, of all the names to remember, Coach Prosser had remembered mine. He kept walking toward me though and said, "Come walk with me for a second, Alan. How 'bout you show me where the locker room is? I haven't seen it yet." I nodded my head, and together we began to walk out of the dimly lit practice gym and down the three flights of stairs. Just Skip Prosser and me. Man to man.

I think I was supposed to be nervous, but for some reason Coach made me feel at ease. "So how did you end up at Wake?" he said. I gave him my history, and in those five minutes, someone made a concerted effort to learn about my life. Part of me knew that he was trying to see what I was about; and as we proceeded into the locker area, I began to wonder if he had pulled me aside to tell me things were not going to work out. Instead we talked about the need for change in our current locker room.

Coach exclaimed, "You guys need to get a PlayStation or something in this joint." A new PlayStation was nice, but even better was the state-of-the-art athletic center which happened to come at the same time as Coach Prosser. I was amazed at his friendliness and down-to-earth nature. Despite his no-nonsense speech the night before, I could tell he was a players' coach. I liked him.

As we walked back up the stairs, I felt privileged to have spent those moments with Coach. He made me feel as if I was going to be the guy that would average twenty points a game next year, when, in reality, I was just the player on the team who could barely grab the rim.

I suppose if I hadn't fared well in those five minutes, I would have never come back up those stairs that day, but I did. As I started to warm up for my three o'clock workout, I tried to remind myself that this was not a personality contest and that the true test would come during the individual workout I was about to go through with the assistant coaches.

Coach Gaudio began the workout by saying that nothing would be done half-speed. Everything was an all-out, 100-percent effort. After lining up at half-court, Coach instructed each of us to "dribble at the chair hard, make an in-and-out move, and then finish with a left-handed lay-up." Mind you, all of this was before Coach Prosser had even given his press conference.

I was third in line at this point. After watching my two teammates go in front of me, I flashed my hands to receive the ball from the coach. But instead of hitting me with the pass, Coach hesitated for a second and said, "Alan, why don't you just pass for me today?" So I left the line along with my pride at half-court and trotted over to where Coach Gaudio was standing. Now it was official: I was the designated passer.

My role was small, but Coach Prosser still noticed me. He said, "Come on, Alan, give me a better pass than that. Pop it in there. They'll catch it if you aim for their face." Though I was merely a passer, I can honestly say that I loved being a small part of this new beginning. It was the first day of the Prosser era, and I was there.

Walking with Coach earlier and seeing the intensity of his assistants during workouts was inspiring. Some coaches refer to the word WIN to mean "Whatever Is Necessary"; and during that first day of workouts, I became determined to do whatever was necessary to get on Coach Prosser's team. I may not have gotten to go through the workouts like the scholarship guys did, but I still got to be a part of them. And I was going to continue to be a part of them. I was not going to go away. I had made up my mind that I was going to go everywhere the team went that spring. If there was a pickup game, I would be there. If there was a meeting, I would be there.

Later that afternoon, all of the players drove over to Bridger Field House to hear Coach Prosser's press conference. With all his players in the room, he made it known to the community that Wake basketball was going to a new level. He said, "Oh, and we're going to win. We are going to win!"

The next day I woke up to read the morning paper and found the whole front page dedicated to Coach Prosser's arrival in the ACC. In the center of the page, there was a blown-up head shot of the new coach as he waited his turn to speak at the press conference. I saw the picture and was immediately reminded of the fact that I was at that press conference too. I say this because, if you looked at the photo carefully, you could see another face directly behind Coach Prosser's. Though it was a bit blurry, you couldn't miss me. *I really was everywhere.*

14

A Long Football Field

I REMEMBER one person from high school very well. His name was Josh. He loved all sports. He was the guy that was always around school throwing or shooting a ball. Josh played football and even got to dress out for the state championship game his senior year.

If you looked at him, you probably wouldn't pick him to be on your team, though. From a physical standpoint, he was way behind everyone else. He wasn't capable of beating out others for their positions. He was tough, however, and in spite of his skeptics, he wouldn't go away. No matter what happened in practice, he always seemed to come back the next day.

In college, I often found myself feeling like Josh because I obviously wasn't as talented as some of my other teammates. I remember especially feeling like this one day when our strength coach took us out onto the football field after weights. Coach Reeves, the new strength coach, made his presence known early as he conveyed to our team that his philosophy on weight training was not what we were accustomed to seeing.

As Coach Reeves huddled us together on the football field, we all noticed the four large wooden sleds sitting in the end zone. Coach said, "With the help of these sleds, we are going to become a more mentally tough basketball team. The drills we're about to do are the drills that are going to pay off in the second halves of your games this year." Apparently, Michigan State had used the same type of sleds, and they were, of course, the defending national champions.

"Why not learn from the best?" Coach said. The sleds were heavy. Three of them weighed nearly 400 pounds each, and the smaller one was at least 150. Coach told us we would pair off and go over to the sleds, where we would each put on one of the two vests that were attached to the hooks on each of the sleds. The light sled only had one vest. He explained that there would be two guys to a sled and that the goal was to sprint and drive your feet as hard as you possibly could so that the sled could pick up speed and make it across the goal line at the opposite end of the field. The first group to move the sled a hundred yards across the finish line "won."

My partner was Darius Songaila, who now plays for the New Orleans Hornets. He was a *little* stronger than I was. I could tell he wasn't thrilled about being my partner, but as I thought about it, I wouldn't have wanted to be my partner in this drill either. We were the third group to race. As we watched the two groups that went in front of us compete, I could tell for the first time that the guys were not easing through this particular drill. They were struggling! You could hear the grunting getting louder as the first two groups made their way across the field. This was quite intimidating to me as I looked down the field, which now seemed more like two hundred yards. Coach looked at me as Darius and I got rid of the slack in our ropes. Right before the strength coach gave the command to go, he said to me, "Buddy, you're going to have to work hard here. Pull your weight."

Then Darius chimed in, "Buddy, you better not stop driving your feet. I'm serious, dude—get it done!"

I nodded my head and got in an athletic stance, made sure I was behind the line, and waited for the go ahead.

"Ready. Go!"

I took off from the starting line, but not really—we weren't moving that fast. I drove my skinny legs into the artificial turf as hard as I possibly could. As I gasped for air, we made our way to the 25-yard line. We kept moving, and I could hear Darius say, "We're almost halfway, Buddy." We continued down the left sideline of the field. I was dying.

At this point, we were slowing down, and I could hear Darius yelling at me, "Come on, Buddy. Quit acting like a freshman. PULL!" Darius obviously failed to take into consideration that I was 85 pounds lighter than he was. I tried, but I was in pain. As we crossed the 50-yard line, I noticed that somehow our sled was now going down the middle of the field instead of down the left sideline as we had intended. We had changed our course. As I kept pulling, I could hear the guys at the end of the field yelling, "Come on, Buddy. Do it. You got this!"

Even though I couldn't feel my legs, I kept pulling. I was as low to the ground as I could get. As we crossed the 25-yard line on the other side of the field, I noticed our sled was moving slower and slower. I also took it as a bad sign that Darius was two yards in front of me. I think we were supposed to be even with each other, but this wasn't the case. Our sled chemistry was off, and by now, our sled was heading toward the right sideline. At this point, I was beginning to see spots. As I closed my eyes, I continued to drive my legs as hard as my body would let them. I couldn't hear anything that my teammates were saying, but I could hear Darius yelling at me, "What are you doing, Buddy. Come on, dude!"

As I opened my eyes I could now see the sideline bleachers. *Wait, I shouldn't be going in the direction of the bleachers. This is not good. We should be going toward the goal line,* I thought as I gasped for air. At this point, our sled came to a temporary stop. We got it going in the right direction, and as we did, I saw that the other group had already finished.

I could hear my teammates again, "Man up, Buddy, man up, dawg." So I decided to *man up* and somehow found within me one last surge of strength. Forty-five seconds later, we got the sled through the last twenty-five yards where we crossed the goal line out of bounds on the right sideline. Someone immediately unhooked my vest, and as I raised my hands off my knees, I realized what had just happened. We had started in the left corner of one end zone, traveled across the width of the field towards the

---

The glory of sport is witnessing a team perform as a single unit striving for a common goal and ultimately bringing distinction to the jersey the players represent.

—DICK VITALE

---

sideline bleachers, and then to the opposite corner of the other end zone out of bounds.

It took me a few minutes to recover. I was so exhausted I ignored my teammates who were still laughing at me. So what if I

needed the entire field to work with? Nobody said we had to go in
a straight line. All I know is that, on a hot summer day in June, my
sled made it across the finish line. And in case you were wondering, I was pulling the right side of the sled.

The next day, we concluded our workout with sled pulling
again. As I noticed none of the players standing next to me, Coach
Reeves gave out the assignments: "All right, here are the pairings.
Get with your partner. Antwan and Darius, Craig and Broderick,
Steve and A.W., Shetzy and Josh, and Buddy, why don't you pull
the single sled today?"

Those were difficult workouts on the football field that summer. They still remind me of my high school friend, Josh. If you
had been at the state championship game in Nashville, Tennessee,
my senior year of high school, like me, you would have noticed
him as he ran out of the tunnel. His hands were deformed and
extended maybe to where the elbow would normally be. He was
still able to sling a football into the air; but in reality, he could
never throw like a quarterback, catch like a receiver, or tackle like a
linebacker.

Despite his lack of ability, Josh would always come back to the
football field each day, and his determination served as an inspiration in my life. This inspiration didn't come when I was
scoring twenty points a game back in high school, but instead
came when I, too, found myself struggling on a football field
among teammates who were all bigger, stronger, and better than
I was.

From a physical standpoint, the sled drills were the hardest
part of my summer. I wasn't very good at them; and rightly so,
nobody wanted to end up with me as their partner. Since I was a
walk-on, I wasn't required to do any of the workouts in the off-

season with the team, but each day I came back to that same football field where I would get hooked up to a sled.

Throughout those weeks at summer school, I got more chances to pull the big sled. By the end of June, the sled I was pulling only needed half of the width of the field to make the 100-yard pull. I may not have been as strong as the other players, but I improved each day. Looking back, I realize the only reason I was able to improve was because certain people in my life showed me that no matter how far my sled went off course each practice, I needed to come back the next day.

SECOND HALF
Walk-on

I didn't know what to give my dad for Christmas. I had already given him plenty of gear in years past. This time, I had to be original.

One day, I went into the coaches' office and asked if they would make me a tape with all of my highlights from the first ten games.

It was one of my dad's favorite Christmas presents ever. After he opened it, we all went upstairs, put the film in, and watched my highlights.

The tape lasted forty-five seconds.

15

Meet Me in My Office

I ALWAYS wondered what my life in college would have been like without basketball. It would have been different: I would have had a lot more time for friends, longer Christmas breaks, and would have gotten more playing time in intramurals. Maybe it would have been easier. Though the challenges of being a walk-on seemed never-ending, I was determined to be a teammate.

As a walk-on, people never really knew my whole story—it never made the paper. People didn't know how I got my uniform; I was just there. So, as fans saw that I was back on the bench again for my sophomore year, it was assumed that my making the team was a "given;" that I smoothly survived the new coaching change. This wasn't the case, though, and as I reflect on my ultimate test as a walk-on, I understand why I valued the team so much: having teammates, traveling, conditioning, and long practices. I appreciated these things because, as a walk-on, I always knew I was only *one visit to the coach's office* away from having my name taken off the roster. For this reason, my most difficult task in the fall of sophomore year was not having to sit on the bench, but keeping my seat there.

On a hot day in June, our team began the summer with a meeting. By incessantly showing up everywhere Coach Prosser went that spring, the coaches decided to include me in the meeting—an invitation that boosted my confidence and security in knowing that I was on the team. As all the players congregated in the film room, Coach Prosser began the meeting by saying, "Players are made in the off-season fellas, and what we do between now and October will determine just how far we go in March."

Coach had a great ability to create the "big picture," and at the beginning of this particular meeting, he did just that. He used the word *critical* to refer to the eight weeks that we would spend away from each other that summer; his philosophy was that a team wins games before the season even starts.

Coach concluded the meeting that day by telling us stories of how his former players often called him up to say how much they missed their playing days. Coach claimed that there was no better place than the gym and that we should be there as much as we could. He would always say, "Fellas, I like gym guys, guys that love to be in the gym."

A few minutes later, Coach added perspective to our off-season, pointing out that he didn't come to Winston-Salem to be good in three years—Coach never liked the term "rebuilding year." He exclaimed, "What's important right now is bettering yourselves so that we can be good now! And don't forget what I said about how lucky you guys are: you get to come to the gym every day. And I'm telling you, fellas," then for a brief second, he smiled and shook his head, "it's the best place to be. Let's be good now. 1...2...3...Wake."

That day, Coach inspired me. Although my role on the team seemed small, the meeting made me determined to be at the top of my game when I came back in August. A little encouragement from the coaches had gone a long way—I was ready to work.

Dad always taught me the importance of writing things down. He drives a lot, and on the dashboard of his car, he keeps a yellow pad on which he writes down his goals and objectives—long-term and short-term. Likewise, I have learned that there is something to seeing your goals on paper. That night I wrote down the areas of my game I wanted to improve, along with another list which outlined how I would do it:

GOALS

1. Gain 5lbs. of muscle; become stronger
2. Get a quicker release on my jump shot
3. Build endurance; be ready for conditioning
4. Become quicker off the dribble
5. Become a better mid-range jump shooter

HOW I WILL ACCOMPLISH THESE GOALS

1. Talk to someone who knows about nutrition, eat better & lift weights 4 times a week. 50 pushups before bed every night.

2. Work on shooting every day (500 shots a day)

3. Get on a running program, combination of distance & sprints.

4. Do a series of full-court dribbling drills & stationary ball-handling drills each day.

5. Force myself to work on mid-range jumper in pickup games.

These were my goals hanging on my bathroom mirror. I looked at them everyday. During that summer, my teammate Steve recorded all of his workouts and food intake, so I decided to buy a notebook and do the same. In sports, I learned that work ethic breeds desire, and charting my progress was a good reminder of how much energy I was exerting in basketball. Seeing improvement was vital to having a greater desire for more improvement.

Talking about getting better was one thing, but doing it was another. I asked a coach from high school to work with me on my conditioning and went to a strength trainer, who had played for the Oakland Raiders and had a knack for getting professional and college athletes ready for their sport. One coach reminded my dad that when I took off my shirt that fall in pickup games, everybody needed to know that I had been working out.

That summer, I poured more into basketball than ever before. When my family was on vacation in Montana, I can remember stopping at small-town football fields and running ladders. Being in shape needed to be a "given," so spending hours and hours in the gym each day was mandatory.

Upon arriving on campus in late August, I ran into some of my teammates: "Look at you, Buddy, you finally got a little bigger. Look, y'all, he's got a few pebbles stickin' out his arm." So I wasn't exactly a rock just yet, but I had improved my body and was in the best shape of my life.

The first few days back were always dedicated to academics. We met with Mrs. Caldwell, our academic advisor, and she instructed us on where to get our books and so forth. The scholarship players, of course, had their books all ready to go in a box at the book store. I was just a normal student—I searched for mine on the shelves.

I always loved the start of a new school year. It was a new beginning: I had a new room, a new dorm, and thankfully, I was no longer a freshman. I knew my way around now and had a new sense of confidence. Everything was starting to fall into place again.

My work ethic throughout the spring semester, summer school, and Coach Prosser's basketball camps had secured my spot on the team. I was even asked to get fitted for my jersey. I looked forward to seeing the coaches as I was now ready to take on the challenges of the preseason.

The first day of class, as I was walking back from lunch, I ran into Coach. He couldn't have been nicer. As I walked away, he yelled back at me, "Hey, Alan, come by my office sometime tomorrow. I wanna talk to you."

Why did he want to talk to me? He had been too nice for it to be anything negative, so that night I went to sleep in anticipation that Coach would outline his expectations for me as a walk-on, and then invite me to be a part of conditioning with the rest of the team.

The next day, I consciously tried to suppress my anxiety as I waited in Mrs. Heflin's office for Coach Prosser to get off the phone. A few minutes later, I heard Coach say, "Send him in." Unassumingly, I walked up to his desk and shook his hand. Coach Prosser was not big on small talk in situations like this. He was a straight shooter. As I sat down in the chair in front of him, he wasted no time in telling me, "Alan, I gotta be honest with you. You still want to walk-on, don't you?"

"Yes, sir, absolutely."

"Well, here's the deal. I've got too many guards, and as a staff, we've decided that we don't need a walk-on at the guard position. We need a bigger player: 6'5", 6'6", a guy that can bang down low with some of these big guys in practice. I know you're a great kid, but as a head coach, my job is to make sure that as a team, we have what we need. And I'm going to have you stop working out with

---

The ultimate measure of a man is not where he stands in moments of comfort and convenience, but where he stands in times of challenge and controversy.

—DR. MARTIN LUTHER KING, JR.

---

the team right now, because the last thing I'm going to do is have you go through the whole preseason and then cut you. That's not fair to you. We might have tryouts in October though, and if we do, you're welcome to do that."

Once again, I was shocked. What about staying up in Winston-Salem for summer school? What about working his camps? What about the sleds? What about getting asked to get fitted for a jersey? What about my teammates who wanted me on the team? What about the hours and hours I had spent in the gym and on the track in July and August? How was this happening again? I knew this was no place for losing my composure, so I thought about what I wanted to tell him as he gave me the bad news. "Coach, to be honest, I'd be willing to go through all of the preseason workouts. And, if in the end, you have to cut me, I'd be willing to accept that. I've been working all summer long for this. I'm willing to do whatever it takes to be on your team."

Then he responded, "Unfortunately, I'm going to have to let Coach Mack make that decision. He's in charge of conditioning, and I just don't know if that would work out. You'd have to talk with him."

At this point, I knew Coach had told me what he needed to tell me. As I began backing up to go out the door, something told me that I couldn't leave that office without telling coach how I really felt. I took a step back towards his desk. I didn't know exactly what to say, but as I desperately looked into his eyes, my heart took over and in a shaky voice I said to him, "Coach, it really meant a lot to me when you talked to us at that first meeting this summer. You talked about how the basketball court was one of the best places you could possibly be and how one day it's going to be over. I just want you to know that with all my heart, I'm not ready to leave the gym yet. I'm not ready for it to be over."

Coach nodded his head, "I understand, Alan."

My words couldn't have been truer. I wasn't ready for basketball to be over. As I made my way out of Coach Prosser's office that day, I refused to believe that I had crossed over the threshold of his door for the very last time.

16

Midnight Madness

AS A LITTLE KID, I was afraid of the dark. Every night before I laid my head down on my pillow I would make sure the door to my lighted bathroom was cracked. I always seemed to be looking for light; and as I began my sophomore year, I was having trouble finding it.

After I heard the disheartening news from Coach Prosser, it was as if there was a cloud of darkness following me everywhere I went. It was hard for me to be away from my teammates. To make things worse, my friends kept reminding me of what had happened:

"How's basketball going, Alan?"

"Well, actually, I'm not really with the team right now, but I think the guys are doing well." I trusted that God was in control, but I would be lying if I said I wasn't struggling with the idea that my basketball career could potentially be over.

Just as Coach instructed me to, I asked one of our assistants if I could participate in conditioning. I was told that there were too many players already running and that there might not be enough lanes on the track for me to fit into the program. To be honest, I don't think my not getting to condition had anything to do with the number of lanes on the track, but rather the fact that the coaches didn't want me to go through a grueling pre-season and then not make the team. There was no time for worrying though.

The only thing I could do at this point was to work out on my own. I could, however, show up at open gym because it was "open gym." Only scholarship players really played but, theoretically, I could be there. Besides, they usually needed an extra when someone got hurt. So, everyday at 4:45 I showed up to GYM 403, where we played most of our pickup games that year.

It was emotionally hard for me to get to these sessions early because the team always conditioned before they played. As I waited outside the gym doors, it was not uncommon for the guys to come out into the hallway for water. I hated it. They would be exhausted, uncomfortable, and gasping for air—almost too tired even to acknowledge me.

"Hey, Buddy, be glad you're not doing this," one of them would mutter.

I *wasn't* glad. I don't care how bad it was; I wanted to be out there running suicides just like they were, but instead I watched as they drank their water for thirty quick seconds before the whistle blew. As they walked back into the gym, I would solemnly sit against the wall, all the while wondering how I could earn the players' respect without going through the pain they went through. There was not a thing I could do.

After the forty-five minutes was up, conditioning would come to an end—that was my sign to walk in for open gym. In most of the pickup games that year, I didn't even get to play. I would sit and watch the entire time, hoping deep down that I might get picked up for a game. I never missed a pickup game that fall, and over the course of that preseason, I sometimes got to play the third game if I was lucky.

Each day I was ready, though. On one particular occasion, our Director of Basketball Operations was playing with us and happened to be guarding me. A few of the scholarship guys were nursing minor injuries at the time. As the gym only had ten players that day, the captains had no choice but to call my name.

As the game got under way, I remember hitting a three while Coach guarded me. Soon after, I hit another. Some of the players on the other team began to comment, "You better guard Buddy." Coach Kelsey, our Director of Basketball Operations, was one of the most competitive people I had ever met and a very solid player. He was twenty-six years old at the time. After I hit the two threes, he began to tense up and guard me even tougher. While I was taller, Coach was definitely stronger and quicker than I was, but that day my shooting ability compensated for my weaknesses. My teammates said, "Do him again, Buddy, do him again!" I pulled up for yet another three. As the ball went through the net, I had earned the right to confidently backpedal down the court. As I did, I'll never forget Josh Howard yelling in the direction of the Coach, "Buddy's doing you up; that's why Buddy needs to be on this team!"

If there was one player that stood up for me during this whole process, it was Josh. He was "the man" and usually coaches listen to "the man." That was a memorable moment, and as the end of the preseason was approaching, I needed more of these moments. The players couldn't have been more supportive. They often encouraged me, patted me on the back, and told me how much they wanted me back on the team. They would say, "Man, Buddy, it wouldn't be the same without you, dawg." In the meantime, I continued working out at night with Steve and A.W. I didn't know if the opportunity to try out was going to come, but if it did, as always, I would be ready.

On a Friday in mid-October, I made my way to lunch in our student center, where I noticed the signs on the windows of the doors. The notices were advertisements for Midnight Madness, to be held that night in Reynolds Gymnasium. According to NCAA rules, Division One teams were not allowed to practice until midnight the next day. As I read the poster, I learned that the doors to the gym on campus would open at 9 P.M. I called my brother Campbell after lunch and told him about the event.

Cam was my biggest fan; and even though I wasn't playing, he still wanted to be there. He had just graduated from college in the spring and was working for Lance Foods in Charlotte. Later that night, he met me on campus. As we met, we saw the line extending nearly a hundred yards out the doors of Reynolds Gymnasium. The line went all the way down the street. Soon after, I got in line with Campbell and my two friends from the golf team, Bill and Cortland.

I had mixed emotions as I waited in line to see the team that night. I was anxious about seeing what the team would look like. But more than that, I was disappointed at the thought of not getting to be a part of it all.

At this point, I had heard nothing about the possibility of walk-on tryouts. I was helpless, and the only thing I could do was watch *my* teammates scrimmage. I wondered how discouraging it would be to watch, as Cam and my buddies inched further toward the entrance to the gym.

Thirty minutes later, along with a thousand other students, I anxiously awaited the arrival of the 2001–2002 men's basketball team. There were all sorts of games to hype up the crowd before the guys made their official entrance. After the student three-point contest ended, midnight approached. The fans were on edge as the lights went out in the small, high school–like gym. The students erupted. After a few more minutes of darkness, the big screens in the middle of the court began to show a highlight tape that one of the local news channels had created. The tape concluded. By now, the gym was louder than ever. The darkness made the roars even more noticeable, and as the man-made fog began to fill the door to the sounds of pump-up music, the countdown started: "10 … 9 … 8 … 7 … 6 … 5 … 4 … 3 … 2 … 1."

The spotlight was now on the entrance to the gym as the team made their way through the fog to the loudest roars of the night. I could feel myself in a trance as I watched the players run around the gym before huddling up.

One of the most difficult moments of my life was watching my teammates jumping up and down at center court. The spotlight shined directly on the players. As I gazed down, I knew exactly what they were saying: "Let's do this. Y'all know what we gotta do. Let's show 'em what we all about for real." I was sitting in the dark; I could see my teammates, but they couldn't see me. Amid the loudest of cheers, I watched silently.

"1 … 2 … 3 … Wake!"—I knew exactly what they were saying as the spotlight showed they were about to break the huddle. That night the lights had gone off in Reynolds Gymnasium. As I watched my teammates run out of the tunnel without me, I feared the darkness I was sitting in. But I could see the light—and that's where I was determined to be.

17

One Last Chance

MIDNIGHT MADNESS left a bad taste in my mouth that didn't leave for days. I wanted my jersey back! Coach Prosser's first practices were well underway by now, and as I began to talk to the players about the first few workouts, I was not surprised at their initial reactions.

A.W. said, "Man, this isn't anything like last year. It was crazy, dude. The clock was on the whole entire time, and I bet we didn't stop for three hours. I've never played so much defense in a practice."

Apparently, the coaches demanded all-out intensity in every drill. Practices at the beginning of the season were always longer, and I eagerly waited to have a chance to be a part of them. I had heard nothing about tryouts at this point, but continued to fine-tune my game.

After class one day that week, I walked to the upper quad of our campus where a number of dormitories enclosed nearly two hundred yards of beautiful lawn graced by magnolia trees. The prettiest site on the quad was Wait Chapel, Wake Forest's signature landmark. As I continued to walk along the path, I slowed down to check my mailbox. As I approached the post office door, I stepped on a notice taped to the ground that read:

WALK-ON TRYOUTS

OCTOBER 26TH

8:00 P.M., MILLER CENTER

OPEN TO ALL STUDENTS

Must have had a physical in the past year

Game on, I thought as I stared at the bulletin. Open tryouts it was; and even though I knew they were looking for a bigger player, I was going! Of all the players there, I would be the most prepared. I had exactly one week to get ready. I was in *good* shape, but after this week, I would be in *great* shape. I would be fresh, rested, and ready to go. The following days would be dedicated to preparation for next Wednesday at 8:00.

The first step in getting ready was to make sure that I ate right. So later that night, I went to the Golden Corral, where I knew I could get a solid meal at a good price. In college, I had friends out-side of basketball—I was a people person, but I was sometimes energized by my solitude. Even my teammate Antwan used to say, "Sometimes you got to have a little me time." More times than not, my "me time" took place at the Golden Corral, my favorite place to eat. My dream was to have my name on a certificate on the bulletin board listing those who had eaten there over two hun-dred times.

One night during that week of tryouts, I showed up as usual by myself. The same server gave me four clean buffet plates and all the fruit punch refills I wanted. I remember getting a little of everything that night. After finishing dinner, I left the table and made my way to the gumball machine, hoping for a red. Later, while in the restroom, I heard, "Alan."

I didn't expect to run into anyone I knew in the Golden Corral men's room. However, to my surprise, there was Coach Battle, Coach Prosser's top assistant. He said, "I just wanted to make sure you heard about tryouts. Don't get frustrated about being in the dark and all. I know how hard it is, not knowing where you stand. I was a walk-on at Marshall. I earned a scholarship and became the captain of the team . . . but I started as a walk-on. It's a tough road. Just keep working hard—that's all I can tell you."

Coach Battle had taken a step out of his way to encourage me and as a result, he made my night. I was pumped up and can remember getting in my car and calling Dad to tell him about the conversation with Coach. The exchange with Coach B would not have been a big deal to most, but it was enough to make me work even harder in the days preceding tryouts. I went straight to the gym that night—I was inspired.

My friends understood what was at stake and began to convey their utmost support. Mike called to ask if he could rebound for me. One day, Bill and Allen kicked balls out to me as I worked on my quick release from the three-point line. Another night, Stephen made pass after pass as I tried to see how many threes I could hit out of fifty. I'd go again if I made fewer than forty—I was not a great defender, but I could shoot.

One time, I took a run through campus and, again, was reminded of my friends' support. It was a Friday night—there was no way I could go out with next Wednesday's tryouts on my mind. As I ran on the walkways around campus, I passed one of the fraternity lounges. Approaching the sidewalk near the party that was going on, a friend recognized me and pointed. I could hear him say, "Y'all, look it's Alan." All of the students began to clap and say things like "You're gonna make it, Alan, you're gonna make it!"

I continued running, and took comfort in the fact that of all the guys trying out, I was the only one getting better that Friday night. Every second that week, I tried to do something that would give me an edge.

The day before tryouts, I had already gone by to tell one of my professors there was no way I could take a Spanish test the day of tryouts. "Muy bien, Alano," he said, agreeing with my desire to concentrate. I would make it up Thursday. When classes were over that day, I ate at the Golden Corral again and, without telling anybody, went to check into the Hampton Inn nearly ten minutes away from campus. I knew this week was business, so I refused to have any distractions the night before tryouts. I also decided not to attend classes Wednesday. The next morning, this was my schedule:

A.M.

9:00:	Wake up
9:30:	Continental breakfast in the lobby
10:00:	Light jog outside
10:30:	Watch *The Price is Right*

P.M.

12:00:	Lunch at the Golden Corral
1:00:	Hard shoot-around at Reynolds Gymnasium
2:00:	Rest
4:30:	Pre-tryout meal at Golden Corral
5:30:	Reynolds Gymnasium; light shoot-around
7:00:	Stretch in hotel room
7:15:	Quiet time; pray that I would relax
7:30:	Read the index card Dad had FedEx'd
7:35:	Drive over to campus
7:45:	Wait for my opportunity

That whole day, butterflies captured my stomach; and as I sat against a wall outside the Miller Center, I felt them more than ever. I expected to be nervous, though. I threw up before playing some of my best games in high school.

Sooner or later, the gym doors opened. As I shot around, I realized nearly twenty-five other guys wanted the spot on the team that I wanted.

Minutes later, all the guys trying out moved over to the bleachers, where Coach Prosser told us what being a walk-on was really like. He said, "I'm telling you, fellas, it's hard." He explained how the tryouts would work. We would warm-up by doing left-handed lay-ups and then play five-on-five for one hour. He told us what he was looking for. We began the lay-ups. I made all of mine; I had already made plenty of lay-ups in Cameron and the Dean Dome— how bad could it be?

My first opportunity came in the second game—I played hard. I picked up my man full-court and guarded him from baseline to baseline. I talked on every defensive possession: "I got your help; I got your help; I got weak side!" At one point, I even took a charge. On my first few shots, however, I knew I was forgetting to slow down and square up. There were moments when I was overwhelmed by the pressure of what I was doing. It was as if my basketball future was riding on sixty minutes of playing—the more I thought about it, it was.

I wasn't pleased with my offensive performance in the first game. However, as I brought the ball up the floor during the second, I forgot about it as I saw the gym doors open. While dribbling down the right side of the floor, I saw a group of guys walk in. I couldn't believe it—it was them! One by one, all of the scholarship players filed into the gym. They came to encourage me. The past year, I had spent hours and hours watching them from the bench. Now, they were the ones on the bench supporting my every move. It was as if their entrance had a calming and motivating effect at the same time.

With my newly found confidence, I knocked down a few threes and aggressively attacked the basket. During that hour, the coaches yelled out to many of the other players when they made a good play, "What's your name, son?" The coaches knew my name well, and I could only hope they would remember it in the days to come. Throughout the tryouts, I protected the ball, ran the floor, made solid passes, and played tenacious defense. At the end of the night, I knew I had done everything possible. I left it all on the floor.

As I ate a snack in the student center later that night, I wondered if, in the next few days, I would be one of two guys to get a phone call from the coaches. At the tryouts there were definitely some bigger and stronger players, but I was not deterred. Other guys played well, but I knew I had played better. Even though I knew they weren't looking for a shooting guard, I hoped my play was too noticeable to ignore.

Nearly two days passed; I had heard nothing! Each night after the tryouts, I called Steve to see if any walk-ons had been asked to come to practice. He told me there hadn't been any so far, so I continued to wait. In the meantime, I let my Spanish professor know I was too preoccupied with basketball to make-up his test. I don't think he liked my doing this again, but I was too anxious to care. I couldn't sleep very well those nights. I learned what it meant to toss and turn as I lay in my top bunk each night, wondering what the coaches were thinking. Was my preparation for that opportunity going to result in success? I didn't know at this point.

Fall break was that weekend; although I hadn't heard, I made no plans to leave campus. Friday afternoon I sat at my desk contemplating whether or not I should begin looking over some grammar for Spanish, but I was interrupted as the phone rang.

"Alan, it's Coach B. Can you be over at the office at one? We need to talk to you."

Coach had spoken to me on the phone in a fairly monotone voice. As I made my way across campus, I began to have the feeling that this was a pity meeting for Alan because the coaching staff felt like they owed me an explanation of why they couldn't invite me back on the team. Despite their hints that they may not have been able to keep me, they still knew how hard I had worked. I suppose I never took hints very well, but I knew they saw my work ethic and heard about it from the other players.

Ten minutes later, I found myself sitting in Coach Prosser's office. One by one, the assistants walked in. They didn't speak as Coach Prosser followed them into the room. I knew what was coming; I knew it. I sat with a stoic face, and as the coaches got situated, the room got quiet yet again. The assistants were waiting for Coach Prosser to speak; and soon after, he said, "Alan, we decided to keep only two players." There was a slight pause. He stuck out his hand. "Congratulations."

I shook Coach's hand. As everything inside my body raced, I began to get chills. I wanted to jump up and give Coach Prosser a hug, but he wasn't exactly the touchy-feely type. I wasn't either, but I could have been at that moment. I kept my cool and suppressed my emotions to a small smile.

I couldn't believe it. Just as I started to smile, one of the assistant coaches said, "I hope you know this is serious stuff." Then another chimed in, "Alan, I don't know what your situation was like last year, but this could be totally different. This is not *Hoop Dreams*. You're never going to play, I promise you. And you probably won't even get to travel. You are going to be on the scout team however long you play." I concurred with everything they were saying. As I walked out of the office, Coach Prosser said, "Alan, don't *mess* it up!"

Upon hearing the good news, I tried to walk into the team's new locker room, but I didn't have a code. I knocked, though, and my teammates let me in. As soon as they saw me, they yelled my name: "Buddy!" I got a few of those handshakes with the hug included, and then heard Josh trot into the training room and yell, "Hey, y'all, Buddy's back. Ha, ha, Buddy is back!"

Later that day, I drove my car down a side street, the same side street I had driven down nearly seven months after getting cut at the end of my freshman season. As I pulled my car off to the side, I thought about what had just happened.

The time between my freshman and sophomore years was tough. However, the challenges during those months paved the way for memories that I could never imagine being without. As I sat in my car even longer, I began to pray. In what seemed like a never-ending battle, God's grace was sufficient for each day. Shortly after, I picked up my phone. I couldn't wait to hear my dad's voice as I heard my phone dialing.

"Hey, Dad."

"What's new with Al?"

"Well, I talked to the coaches today."

"How did it end up?" he asked in an anxious tone.

As Coach Prosser did, I paused for a second, then calmly said, "Number twenty is back!"

That day, I learned that life really is a long-distance race and that sometimes we have to persist, even in the midst of unlikely circumstances. At 2:00 that afternoon, I had crossed over the threshold of Coach Prosser's office door once again. Three minutes later, I got my jersey back. I never took it off again.

TEAM MEETING
Much More Than a Game

As a freshman walk-on, you just don't expect to be up thirty points on Kansas at home, but we were. The Jayhawks were ranked #6 in the country at the time. So, as I checked in, I made sure I brought my A game. With a minute left, I surprised everyone as I snow-birded down the court and caught a pass for a rim-rattling lay-up—the beginning of a long road trip back to Lawrence for the Jayhawks.

As the crowd rushed the court at the sound of the buzzer, I was in awe. For five minutes, I partook in the celebration with the rest of our fans. Everyone was crowded around me. Why? Because I was the only player that was still on the court. I didn't know the team had already gone into the tunnel.

With much fear, I opened up the locker room door; the players and coaches were staring at me. Realizing that I had been gone, Coach looked at me and said, "Who do you think you are?"

I didn't say anything back, but I thought, My name is Buddy, and I just scored against Kansas.

18

Picture of Hope

During my high school career, my winter job was to referee church league basketball games on Saturday mornings. I usually had eight to ten-year-old boys and was always surprised at the comments often directed at me from the stands. I blew my whistle as fairly as I could, but parents still yelled, "Call a foul. You're terrible, ref—I can't believe you're getting paid."

The little kids seemed to have a great time, so it was disappointing to see parents going ballistic in the stands over their children getting handchecked in the backcourt. The gyms were small, and anything derogatory that was said could be heard loud and clear.

One Saturday, there was a time-out on the floor when a parent began to unleash on me. I think the father had been keeping his kid's stats on his Palm Pilot during the game, so I wasn't all that stunned by his behavior. He said, "Ref, you're a disgrace. I mean, call the game both ways. This is ridiculous—you haven't called one foul on this end the whole third quarter."

I was seventeen years old and was getting paid six dollars per hour. I had never been to referee school, but I did know, in a league where kids only cared about the Gatorade they got at the end of the game, parents shouldn't be acting like this. After the man's remarks, I thought about walking over to the sideline, taking off my whistle, and saying, "Here you go, sir, you take the whistle. You be the ref…go ahead."

That particular incident leads me to address an overriding problem in youth sports today. Parents need to lighten up. I look back at my friends who were the stars in elementary and middle school. They had a lot of talent, but their dads coached every single one of their teams. These parents forced their sons to go to personal trainers and sent them off to as many basketball camps as possible during the summer.

Adding to the intensity, some of their dads even made spreadsheets at work in order to keep up with their kids' stats. A dad shouldn't know that his fourth grade son is shooting 74 percent from the free throw line. No wonder some of my teammates used to tell me they got scared when their dads walked into the gym. And that's a problem—I know this because many of my friends became ambivalent toward the pressure that followed from their parents' living vicariously through their sports careers.

Throughout the years, I never lost my passion for basketball, and I think a lot of that had to do with my parents. As far as my mom was concerned, she always thought I "did great out there." She was a great team mother and, over the years, drove me to hundreds of sporting events. Mom didn't have a clue about the pick n' roll, but she knew how to be an encourager and always listened to me when I was down. Beyond that, I know my mom prayed for me daily. I love my mom.

In my days of playing YMCA and church league as a kid, my

dad never pushed me. He had played in college and was passion-ate about the game, but he never told me to go work on my jump shot. Basketball was *my* deal, yet I was able to share it with him because he let me love the game on my own. I don't think I ever saw my dad at one of my practices. He always let that be *my* time; and after games, he would tell me what I did well and would

---

It's up to us to keep our perspectives and our priorities in order. Let the kids play the games. We had our childhood. It's our kids' childhood now. It's time for us to simply let them go out and watch them enjoy themselves.

—CAL RIPKEN, JR.

---

maybe mention a particular play—if *I* felt like it. He was in my corner and always stayed positive.

My dad was a great encourager—never critical. Between coaches and friends, there was plenty of that already. Dad was my best rebounder, and beyond that, the most amazing man I've ever met in my life. Part of this is because of my mom, but more than anything, the Lord is the one leading his life. Dad possesses a unique ability to be bold and humble at the same time. He's able to make decisions and be firm in what he believes, yet still gra-ciously deal with the people that come in and out of his life.

My dad doesn't like to rush. He drives everywhere; he says he likes to see what's between point A and point B. He knows that sometimes you have to slow down and that everyone should have room for margin in life. And he understands what's important. I know this because I talk to him on the phone everyday—he always answers.

While on a mission trip to Ukraine in 2001, I spoke with Andre, one of the Ukrainian boys who attended our basketball camp. From the "cabin times" we had with the boys before going to bed each night, I gathered that Andre was still wrestling with certain issues. He was unsure about a lot of things.

Late one night, as we walked along the path back to the sleeping quarters, Andre began to ask me some questions in broken English: "Alan, I no understand why God let bad things happen to good people. Me grandfather died in country's war. If God is good, why he let happen?"

To be honest, I was taken aback by his inquiry. While I, too, wrestled with this question, never before had I been responsible for giving the answer. This was the best I had to offer: "You know, Andre, we talked last night in our cabin about how Jesus died on the Cross for our sins. Jesus was good, really good—he was perfect, yet he still became our sin on the Cross. Why did the Son of God have to suffer the worst possible death if he never did anything wrong? How is that fair?"

Andre looked at me, and it seemed as if he really couldn't respond as he thought about what I had said. Then he said, "If Jesus no die, then nobody be saved at all."

"Exactly, so God had a plan . . . and beyond that, Andre, as sinners, you and I don't deserve anything anyway."

Initially, I may have been struck by Andre's question. I still knew the answer, but did I really believe it?

Two weeks later, my family returned from the mission trip only to find out shocking news. On July 22, 2001, my dad returned to Dallas and was diagnosed with leukemia. Why was this happening? Of all people to get cancer, why my dad?

I wish that Andre and I could have talked again at this point, because the explanation I had given an inquisitive Ukrainian boy one night was now being tested. Now, *I* was the one who was being tempted to say that something "bad" was happening to a "good person." I was the one questioning God's sovereignty.

The setback in my family made me pensive. As I looked for encouragement in a disheartening situation, I found it in a surprising place. While my family remained apprehensive, Dad reminded us that weakness is the place we experience God's strength. Upon receiving the bad news, I remember Dad saying, "I look forward to seeing how God will use this cancer in my life and in the lives of others."

In the middle of my senior season, Dad was forced to begin treatments at M.D. Anderson Cancer Center in Houston. Throughout this time, my mom told us how he often reacted to certain medicines he took; his skin would break out in hives, and his blood pressure would get so low that it would cause uncontrollable shaking. On these nights, he could not even fall asleep.

I'll never forget talking to him on the phone the day after one of his worst treatment sessions, one that had lasted nearly fourteen hours. I couldn't help but be nervous as my mom handed over the phone to him in his bed.

What should I ask him, I thought.

"Hey, Dad."

Amid his painful and weary state, Dad said immediately, "Hey, Al. Did you knock a few shots down *in warm-ups* last night?" That was the selfless nature of my dad for you.

Around the same time as my dad's treatments that senior year, we happened to play UNC. Chapel Hill was always my favorite road game, so my last trip to the Dean Dome was most memorable. It was our first ACC game of the year. We were highly ranked at the time, and so was UNC. Beyond a rivalry surrounded by tradition, this night would be the first time we would face off against the most recent newcomer to the ACC, Roy Williams.

The audience was unfairly divided—22,000 fans wearing blue and 300 wearing black and gold behind our bench. The game was nationally televised, and served as the kickoff to FOX Sunday Night Hoops. I could feel the electricity as I warmed up.

After the shoot-around, the team reassembled in the locker room. Coach gave a pregame speech—one for the ages. Scott Prosser, Coach's son, had been developmentally challenged since his youth. But he never missed a game and was the Demon Deacons' biggest fan. One time, Scott even felt it was necessary to jump over the bench to join our huddle during a critical time-out at the end of a game—he needed to remind his dad it was time to press.

After going over the game plan for the final time, the team "took a knee" to say the Lord's Prayer. This particular night, Coach told us that he wanted us to think about the person who had influenced our lives the most. The locker room was silent as he stared us in the eyes and said in a most convincing tone, "You think about it, right now. Who is your hero, fellas? Who is it . . . who helped get you here?" After a short pause, he continued, "Well, whoever it is, that's who I want you to play for. That's who I want you to think about when your back is against the wall tonight." Coach went on to say that his hero was his son Scott. It was the only time in three years that I heard Coach's voice crack—he was about to cry. At this point, I had the chills like I never had before. I could have dunked a basketball right then; I know I could have. With my hero in mind, I was ready to go.

Many say that Wake Forest vs. UNC that night was the greatest regular season game in the history of the ACC. I can't tell you how many lead changes there were. And I can't tell you how many great plays were made. It was basketball at its finest!

It took three overtimes that night to determine a winner; and fortunately, the Deacons came out on top. As I reflect on that game, I remember a team that was motivated to play extraordinary basketball. I, of course, never got to play that night; but as I sat in my seat near the end of the bench, I still thought about my

---

Everything God sends into our lives must be necessary.
Everything he doesn't send must not be necessary.

—JOHN NEWTON

---

hero. In fact, I had been thinking about him all season—for my hero's capability of impacting my life extended way beyond an inspirational speech before a big game.

You see, going into practice each day, I often felt tired, nervous, and discouraged; it was a long season. And if you had told me what the scout team did each day in practice and that I would have to do it six hundred times over four years, there is no way I could have stuck with it. So that senior year, I always followed the same routine before practice: I walked into the locker room and put on my practice gear. As I laced up my shoes on my stool, I always gazed at the 3 x 5 picture taped to the wood paneling of my locker. I stared at it, and then I read the verse written at the bottom: "Consider it pure joy, my brothers, whenever you face trials of many kinds, because you know that the testing of your faith develops perseverance. Perseverance must finish its work so that you may be mature and complete, not lacking anything"

(James 1:2–4). And then I read the words written in black marker at the bottom of the picture, "One day at a time"—because that's all I could do, and that's all my hero could do, too.

During my college career, there were a lot of rough days, a lot of days where I wanted to throw in the towel. But thankfully, the person I had my arm around in that picture always seemed to give me a boost. Like I said, that senior year, I didn't just think about my hero before the *big games*—I thought about him before *every practice*. I love my dad.

19

Skip into Reality

"LET ME tell you something, fellas. Getting playing time from me isn't like Halloween. Just because you put on a suit, that doesn't mean you get candy."

Over the years, I didn't get a lot of *candy*, but I always enjoyed Coach Prosser's wit. I remember the day he came up to me while I was stretching before practice and said, "Alan, I was eating lunch on campus today, and a couple of students asked me the funniest question."

"What's that, Coach?"

"They asked me if there was any way you could get more playing time."

Coach could humble me like this without even cracking a smile. Obviously, I spent hours and hours on the sidelines watching Coach Prosser's ways. I noticed little things about him that probably no one else would; and over three years, I think I learned why Coach Prosser was successful. In addition to sur-rounding himself with the best staff, Coach had a unique ability to motivate players not only for games, but also for practices. He knew how to maximize each player's ability while simultaneously ensuring they understood their roles from a team standpoint. Coach let his "players be players." He recognized their talents and let them play according to their strengths, but stressed that their

---

My responsibility is to get my 25 guys playing for the name on the front of their uniform and not the one on the back.

—TOMMY LASORDA

---

intentions for scoring and fast-breaking were all for the better-ment of one name—Wake Forest. The name on the front of the jersey was more important than the name on the back!

He was demanding, yet knew when he needed to be positive. He was our toughest critic and biggest encourager at the same time. One aspect of his personality I admired most was that every time Coach Prosser stepped on the court, his demeanor was full of energy and emotion. He never let up; sometimes our hardest practices followed our greatest victories. Whether it was a walk-thru, free throw practice, or the tip-off against St. Joseph's in the Sweet Sixteen, Coach was excited about what we were doing.

I respected the fact that he started his coaching career from scratch. Soon after his days of playing basketball at the Merchant Marine Academy, Coach became a history teacher at a high school in Wheeling, West Virginia. He began as a football coach and somehow ended up coaching basketball. As a high school coach, he won a state championship and after that became an assistant under Coach Gillen at Xavier. Eventually, he got his first Division One coaching job at Loyola College (a team that had only one victory the year before his arrival), where he took them all the way to the NCAA Tournament in his first year.

After much success at Xavier, Prosser finally found his way into the ACC. He always reminded us that, before the days of driving his big Mercedes, he was a high school coach painting houses in the summer to make extra money. Coach never forgot where he came from and always encouraged us to do the same. Someone once told me that if you really want to know what a coach is like, ask the guy sitting on the end of the bench. Take it from that guy—Skip Prosser was an excellent coach.

Before a big game one time, he said to us, "Remember where you were just four months ago, fellas— waking up at 5:30 in the morning to run suicides and 440s around the track. You remember how it felt: the sweat, the pain. Why did you do it, fellas, why did you do it? You did it because of this moment that is right before you. That's why you worked so hard and don't forget it. Remember where you were."

Each day before practice, Coach tried to put into perspective whatever we were trying to do. He also had a favorite acronym for the word WIN: "What's Important Now." Every day, Coach utilized the dry-erase board in our practice gym, pointing out "what was important now." He started every practice talking about academics: "Go to your tutors, meet with your teachers, do the things that you need to do to be successful in your classes."

Coach loved history and often encouraged us by using famous quotes from Winston Churchill or Ralph Waldo Emerson. One time, he didn't feel like we were playing hard enough, so he put the number 211 on the board. He asked, "Know what this number represents?" It was quiet for a second; nobody knew the significance of 211. Then Coach went on to tell us that 211 was one degree below 212—the point at which water begins to boil.

Then he said to us, "Right now you guys are playing well, but I need you to take your level of intensity up one degree. If we do that, that's when we'll begin to play at the level we need to play at to make a run at the Final Four." During the time I played for Coach Prosser, it was as if each day he had our team take a step back to gain perspective so that, eventually, we could take a step forward.

At the beginning of Coach Prosser's first year, we won our first two rounds of the Preseason NIT. We squeaked by UNC-Wilmington at home and went down to Fayetteville, Arkansas, where we beat Nolan Richardson's Razorbacks. Those victories earned us a spot in the semifinals of the famed preseason tournament held in Madison Square Garden.

We beat Fresno State in the first round, but fell short against Syracuse in the championship game. While playing in the Garden was a memorable experience, the most meaningful time came when Coach Prosser had our bus driver take us to Ground Zero. As our team pulled up to where the Twin Towers once were, 9/11 became a reality as our team stared tragedy in the eye. We quickly gained a different perspective on the basketball tournament we were playing. It was just a game—really.

Later in my career, Coach Prosser took us to see some kids in the hospital whose lives seemed to be at another type of Ground Zero. A high school basketball team from New York was traveling back home from a tournament in the Carolinas, when a truck hit their van. It was a Saturday, and we had just finished practice. We were playing Clemson the next day, but even so, Coach suggested some of us go see the three injured players.

Upon arriving, the coach of the high school team met us in the lobby of the hospital and brought us up to speed on the players' conditions. Within five minutes, we were around the beds of the injured players, where we gave them t-shirts and other gear. Coach Prosser encouraged each of the kids we saw that day with a few of his own words and then asked me to pray as we all circled around their beds.

I prayed that each of the athletes would rest easy as they slept, that the Lord would give them fast recovery, and that God would be the constant during this setback in their lives. It was obvious by the smiles on their faces; their day had been brightened.

The next day, Coach gave his pregame talk minutes before tip-off. He reminded us of the kids that we had seen in the hospital the day before. Though I received no playing time against Clemson that day, I was thankful that the Lord had blessed me with the ability to run out to give my teammates a "five" during the

Teach us to number our days
so that we may gain a heart of wisdom.

—PSALM 90:12

time-outs. That day I was thankful for the little things; things that once seemed meaningless now seemed meaningful.

On another occasion, Coach had a man come speak who was preparing to relocate to Iraq as a member of the ground forces. My teammate Steve Lepore had a brother who was stationed on a ship for an entire year. It's easy to take for granted, but Coach often reminded us of the freedom for which our troops fought. A basketball game is not a war.

Coach knew that his coaching career started from scratch. From the ground up, Coach made it to the mountaintop of college basketball, yet he didn't seem to forget that some people's lives were stuck at Ground Zero. As Coach continued to try and win more basketball games on the sidelines, he remembered there were valiant soldiers fighting to protect our freedom on the front lines.

My favorite teaching tool that Coach used came after we lost three games in a row. Coach was frustrated with the way we had been playing, but by no means had he given up on us. We were his team, he would say. In one practice shortly after this string of losses, Coach brought a ladder to the court. The ladder had seven steps, each rung representing one of the seven teams we would be playing down the stretch of conference play.

Coach explained that we had to climb the ladder; but in order to get to the top, we had to take the bottom step first and so on. At a low point in the season, the symbolic nature of the ladder proved to be effective. We ended up winning six of our last seven games, finishing third in the conference.

Coach Prosser knew exactly how many games we had left in the regular season that year, but I've learned that in the ladder of life, we don't know how many rungs we have left.

In life, there are no guarantees. We live in a world where airport security sometimes fails, where cancer intrudes, and where swerving across a yellow line often ends in tragedy.

For these reasons, I pray that I will climb my ladder one step at a time and that, along the way, I won't forget to recognize the blessings of each day.

In the midst of success and the constant pressures of his job, I admired how Coach Prosser not only remembered where he came from, but also took a step back to give perspective to every-day life.

He was the best teacher I ever had.

THE LOCKER ROOM
Teammates

One day, Chris Paul and Justin Gray asked me if I would take them to the driving range. It was their first golf outing. As they worked on their iron game beside me, I decided to pull out the driver. On my first swing, I caught the toe and hit a 250-yard drive out to the right. I knew it was ugly, but my teammates were amazed anyway.

Chris said, "Whoa! You see that, J-Gray? Buddy, let me try the 'big boy' right quick." Hesitantly, I handed C.P. my driver and watched him struggle to make good contact. He looked back at me and said, "Man, Buddy, how'd you do that?"

I think it was good for Chris—now he knew how I felt every time I stepped on the court.

20

Everybody on the Line

"HEY, Bo, you had any bites?"

"Not really, but they're starting to rise over here. I just put on an Elk Hair Caddis."

As I watched the light bounce off the boulder directly above the pool in the river, I realized that, regardless of how many brown trout I caught, there was no way that I could possibly have a bad day on the Smith River. Wading in a river set in the middle of a canyon was a beautiful site. As my brother and I waited patiently for a strike one late summer afternoon, I began to rehash my sophomore season. I thought about the new identity that Coach Prosser had instilled in Wake Forest Basketball. Coach always told us that we were going to be known as a hard-nosed bunch of guys. He explained that anyone from Pittsburgh, like him, had to be tough.

A team had to be especially tough when dealing with the injuries we had that year. Injuries can change the dynamics of a team more than anything. I remember when Cincinnati was supposed to go all the way one year, but Kenyon Martin went down in the first round.

As for our team, Steve Lepore, our three-point specialist, seriously injured his knee in Charlotte at the ACC Tournament. Josh Howard had to play through pain much of the season after a nagging ankle injury. And with only minutes to go in the first round of the NCAA Tournament out in California, Craig Dawson separated his shoulder—one of the determining factors as we found ourselves only a rebound and a put-back away from advancement.

Injuries were always prevalent, and some players spent more time in the training room than they did in actual practice. G.C. was the best trainer in the ACC—we all liked being around him; but unfortunately, we had no choice. Coach P demanded toughness. He would say, "Don't get hurt!" If guys were sick, then he'd simply say, "Get more rest and drink more orange juice." And if you were injured, you better have shown up for treatment. Coach would say, "If you're hurt and you don't get treatment, then you're selfish."

All of this is to say, one cannot underestimate the importance of a healthy team in college basketball. You can have all of the McDonald's All-Americans in the country; but if they're not healthy, it doesn't matter. One way to ensure a healthier team was to be well conditioned.

After releasing a nice-sized fifteen-inch rainbow trout into the water that summer afternoon, I realized while the fishing was relaxing, I was only a month away from what I knew would be one of the toughest months of the year: the four weeks in which we conditioned. During that time, our team was expected to move much faster than the current I was standing in that day on the river.

The coaches had told the scholarship guys not to come back in the fall unless they could run a 6:15 mile. When I returned from the river that night, I went upstairs and, instead of my usual Dr. Pepper and chocolate brownie with ice cream, I settled for water and a piece of fruit. The next day I ran hills in the high altitudes of the

---

Players are made in the off-season.

—SKIP PROSSER

---

nearby mountains and did a series of push-ups and lunges. There was no time for slacking off if I was going to be ready.

After the first day of running that fall, I realized why I had feared conditioning, as I was sprawled out in the stall on the bathroom floor. We had just finished a circuit, a number of "seventeens," and suicides—I didn't want anyone to see me. As I sat on the white tile, I could feel the blood rushing to my head and began to see spots. Five minutes later, I got up off the ground only to throw up in the toilet in front of me.

I was shot, and as I washed out in the sink, I could see the circles under my red eyes. One of my teammates came into the bathroom and saw me. I could hear him run out the door saying, "Hey, y'all, Al Will tossin' his cookies in the bathroom!" As I went home later that night, I was discouraged when I remembered what Coach Mack had said at the end of the workout: "This was a light day, fellas. Get plenty of rest."

Thankfully, the next day was much better, mainly because we were on the track, and I was a decent long-distance runner.

Besides Vytas and Trent, I was one of the fastest milers. In my two years of conditioning, I was able to get my mile time down to 5:11.

As the first week came to a close, each of us was given an envelope containing an evaluation form along with a grade that was supposed to be reflective of our performance thus far. I received an 80, the third best. Even though the workouts in the gym had been tough and running twenty suicides in twenty minutes was a challenge, I made most of my times. It was just that it took more out of me to make those times than it did some of the other guys. Just get it done, though, right? Nobody said it had to be pretty.

I'll never forget one of our 6 A.M. workouts during the third week of conditioning. Steve, Josh, and I were all neighbors, so after a small cup of orange juice and a slice of bread, we all drove over together in my car. It was 35 degrees outside and dark as we waited for Coach Mack to walk out of his office onto the track. As we tried to loosen up, you could hear everything from obscenities to groans. We didn't want to be there.

The door to the office finally opened and we saw Coach Mack walk out with his whistle, stopwatch, and clipboard in hand—my stomach always got tight whenever I saw him walking towards the track. Coach glanced over the group to make sure we were all there, and someone said, "Where is Big E?" Eric was a freshman, and naturally all eyes turned toward his roommate to see where he was. Justin said, "He was still sleeping when I left!"

A freshman mistake had been made that day: the roommate had left the room to go to conditioning without his roommate. Unbelievable, I know; but it happened. Moments later, Coach Prosser got out of his car with his Dunkin' Donuts coffee in hand. You could see the dismay come over his face when he discovered that not everyone was there at 6:00 A.M. sharp.

Coach began to lecture, "How much do we ask of you fellas? I mean, really; we ask that you go to class, come to workouts, and that you be on time wherever you're going. And what do I say? 'If

---

In the U.S. Marine Corps, if one guy messes up,
every person in the platoon hikes at 5:00 A.M.

—DEAN SMITH

---

you can't be on time, then be early.' I'm not going to deal with this anymore, fellas. It's gotta stop. Coach Mack, you got them!" Coach Prosser was a players' coach, but he didn't tolerate being late. I knew Coach was right that morning, but I hated the consequences. Thankfully, while we were stretching, the freshman showed up.

After finishing our stretching, we ran a warm-up lap. I feared what we were about to do. Huddling-up with my team, I could see my breath as Coach Mack began to express his displeasure in our lack of punctuality. He said in a condescending voice, "I'm tired of this *stuff*. This won't happen again, fellas. Right now, you're all going to run a 400, guards first in 1:00, big guys in 1:08. Then you're going to get a thirty-second rest, and then you're going to do it again in under 1:02. Then you'll get another thirty-second rest, and you're going to do it under 1:04, and then rest again, followed by another 400 under 1:08. We have four 400s, fellas; and for every one you don't get, you're going to do another one." As I heard Coach Mack, I thought, *This is impossible. This is like running a 4:14 mile with a few seconds of rest in between.*

Coach Mack's running schedule that day *was* impossible—and

it was supposed to be; we were late. The team didn't make their times—not the guards, not the big guys. Consequently, we all ran extra laps; and in the end, Coach Mack issued the final ultimatum. Keep in mind, we were all spent from the 400s we had already run. As we displayed our exhaustion, Coach said, "Get your hands off your shorts. You all still aren't making your times, so here is the deal: everyone has to run one 800 in under three minutes. That's two laps under two minutes and thirty seconds. Big guys, guards, everybody together. If one guy doesn't make it, we all do it again. And I got all day—trust me!"

We were all dragging at this point, but in my mind, I knew I could manage to get around the track twice in two and a half minutes. It was a reasonable pace, but I knew it would still be tough considering what we had already done: "We can do this, fellas. Let's go." I was a walk-on, but I wasn't afraid to be vocal in conditioning.

"Let's do this," Taron said.

"Stay with us, Justin. Come on, man; and Big E, you got this. Let's go," someone else yelled.

"Ready! Go!"

We were off. Everyone made it through the first four turns. As we crossed the halfway point, I could hear Coach Mack call out the times: "Let's go, fellas. Pick it up. You're not gonna make it."

We all kept going as most of us had passed the second turn on the second lap. A few seconds later, we passed the 200-yard marker, approaching steadily on the third turn. As we did, Trent, Taron, and I looked back to see where the rest of the guys were. All were close behind with the exception of Big E. He was trudging along nearly 25 yards behind. All the while, I could hear Coach yelling, "One minute; you better get on it; you guys aren't gonna make it."

Individual running skills didn't matter at this point—it was all about the team getting across the finish line. We had to do something as we looked back in frustration. That's when somebody shouted out, "We gotta get behind those guys in the back; get behind them and get them across!" With that, some of us began to slow our pace to go back to where Big E was. We got on all sides of him—a few of us behind him and the others beside him on his right side.

He said, "Get away, go on, go on."

We said, "No way, man; we're going together."

Coach said again, "You're not gonna make it; hurry up; forty seconds." By now, we literally had hands on his back as we yelled at him to speed up. Together, we approached the final turn and again heard the words, "You better sprint...you better speed it up. Ten ... nine ... eight ... seven ... six ... five ... four ... three ... two ..."

In spite of thinking we couldn't do it, we made it! We began to yell. We yelled because we *all* made it across the finish line— together.

As teammates at Wake Forest, we always ran behind each other— and it didn't stop on the track.

I'll never forget when Jamaal's mom passed away my sophomore year. I can still picture Jamaal crying at his stool as we huddled around his locker a few days after. As tears ran down his face, I looked to my right and saw Josh Howard. He was crying too—he was crying because his teammate was crying.

Another time, we were playing at Maryland my junior year. We were not expected to win, but we hung tight the whole game. With only a few seconds left in regulation, Josh got hold of a loose ball and signalled to the referee for a time-out we didn't have. Minutes later, Josh was crying at his stool, and again we huddled around the teammate who was hurting. That's what we did—we were teammates.

21

New Pair of Shoes

BILL HAAS was an All-American and one of the best golfers ever to play at Wake Forest. We were roommates and loved each other's sports. Bill loved to go up to the gym with me at night and shoot hoops, and I could never stay away from the range.

Bill hit the golf ball effortlessly, and I was always amazed at his laid-back nature. Whether he was in a tournament or just playing a few holes with me, he was relaxed. He'd just go up to the ball and hit it. I'd ask him, "Bill, what do I need to do?"

"Just hit it," he would say. He wasn't an analyzer or the type of player to have a bunch of swing thoughts; he was just Bill. I remember some of the exchanges we would have when he came home from a tournament. I would ask, "Hey, Billy, how'd you hit it?"

"Actually hit it okay today, Al Will."

"How did you end up?"

"I won."

Bill was humble when it came to his golf. If you approached

him at a tournament, he might talk to you for ten minutes. Bill's dad is Jay Haas, a long-time member of the PGA Tour. At fifty years old, he's playing some of the best golf of his life.

When I was a junior, I had a chance to go to Bill's house in Greenville, South Carolina. Right before I walked upstairs to go to bed, Jay said to me, "Hey, Alan, we're going to play nine holes early in the morning before breakfast. It's going to be cold and early; we'll be playing pretty fast. You'd probably rather sleep. But if you wanna come, you're welcome to." He was awfully nice to include an amateur like me, but I could tell that I wasn't going to break his heart if I didn't come along. I couldn't pass up the offer, though: "I'll be there."

We woke up the next morning at 6:30 to be the first group off the tee. Even though I could have used a little practice, we didn't hit any range balls. I suppose Jay, Bill, and Jay Jr. knew their swings well enough to do that sort of thing. As I stood on the back of the #1 tee box, I watched three perfect drives go straight down the long par four, and then came my turn. I had my three wood in hand. As I put my tee in the ground, I noticed the tee boxes we were playing from were called the "Haas Tees," the tees that you play only if you're good. Aligning my shoulders with the target, I thought about three things:

1. There are three Haases behind me.
2. It's a long way to the hole from the tips.
3. Please don't shank it, Al.

I took a deep breath and hit my tee shot. As I tracked down the ball in the air, Jay said, "Go ahead and take another one there, Alan." So I needed a mulligan.

I don't know if having Bill as my roommate inspired me to play great golf, but it did inspire me to play a lot of golf. I loved hitting range balls with the guys and occasionally played with Richard, a 6'5" guard from Mt. Airy, North Carolina. My only teammate who took golf as seriously as I did was Steve Lepore. He was about a thirteen handicap with a slice that took at least seventy-five yards off of every drive he hit. Steve was crafty, though, always referring to his putter as his "magic stick." It was not uncommon to see Steve's whole body lying flat on the ground behind his ball while reading putts—that was Steve for you.

Unfortunately, Steve was never able to fully recover from the injury he received the end of his junior year. He played a big role in our run to the ACC Championship his final season but was sidelined by his knee injury for several games.

Steve was definitely not healthy enough to play against Florida State. As we got off the plane, I couldn't believe how we had gone from thirty-five-degree weather in Winston-Salem to seventy-five in Florida. On the way back from the shoot-around the next morning, Steve and I began to talk golf.

Steve said, "Man, don't you know there are some nice courses around here!"

"Yeah, you know there are. Why don't we go play?" I said.

"I'll do it. It's noon right now; pregame meal is not until 5:30."

"Whatever, man. You'll never go."

"Yeah, I will. Let's do it."

With that, we went up to the room, changed into our khakis we had worn at dinner the night before, called a cab, rented some clubs; and within thirty-five minutes, we were on the first tee at Seminole Golf Club. At 5:15, we returned to the Radisson, went up to our rooms, changed into some practice shorts and t-shirts, and arrived on time to pregame meal—time management at its best.

Steve and I loved golf. Sometimes we even woke up at 6 A.M. to play eighteen holes before class. The summer after my junior year, Steve and I made our way down to Panama City Beach for a church-sponsored summer beach conference where we played even more golf. Steve was a year older than me, so this particular trip would be one of our last chances to hang out for a long time. While the golf was certainly a hook for Steve, I was surprised at his willingness to come along to a conference where our faith would be challenged each morning at various seminars put on by campus ministers from across the country.

That entire year, I had taken my teammate along with me to the ministry I attended each week. We always arrived thirty minutes late because Steve didn't feel comfortable singing the worship music prior to the talk. Upon arrival, we heard Kevin Teasley, our campus minister, give a sermon. Kevin's messages were not predicated on checklists of how to be "good," but were focused on how we all desperately needed Christ in our lives—having a faith in what Jesus did for us on the cross was the only thing that could bring about fulfillment and change in our lives.

Steve always told me he thought he wasn't good enough for God. That year though, I began to share with Steve what Jesus had graciously done in my life and how none of us were good enough for God. Steve was always receptive, but I wondered how his own life would be affected.

I thought time was running out: he was a senior and was leaving soon. I clearly overestimated my role. I knew this because I often talked to Kevin about what kinds of questions I should be asking Steve. Each time, Kevin made a few suggestions, but ulti- mately reminded me that Steve's coming to know the Lord was not dependent on me. He reminded me that it was about the work that God had already begun. Kevin would always say, "Pray for him, Alan. Don't give up on him, man."

People may refuse our love or reject our message, but they are defenseless against our prayers.

—RICK WARREN

Throughout that year, I prayed the Lord would do a mighty thing with Steve's heart. In time, Steve began to see that his faith didn't work like his jump shot. If Steve's jumper was off, he would just practice until it was better. He spent hours and hours perfect- ing his form and improving his timing, so that a three-pointer essentially became muscle memory. Steve was caught in the trap of thinking that he could fix his life like he could fix his jump shot—just make it better. In reality, only God can change hearts.

When I think about Steve's story, and even mine, I often think about basketball shoes. During my senior year, there must have been fifteen pairs of Nikes in my locker. When I played YMCA basketball as a little kid, I only received one pair of shoes per year. So, I wanted to make sure my shoes stayed perfectly clean. I tried to keep them white as long as possible. Whenever they got dirty or scuffed, I took a toothbrush at night and cleaned them with soap and shampoo. I realized quickly; however, it was impossible to keep my shoes spotless, because each time I shot in the driveway, they'd get dirty again. Eventually, I gave up and realized my only hope for a clean pair of high-tops was for my dad to buy me a new pair.

During a twelve-hour car ride on the way home from Florida, Steve decided that he was tired of trying to cover up the scuff marks of his life. And he was tired of trying to make himself worthy before the Lord. After coming to a number of dead ends like these, Steve was shown that he couldn't achieve righteousness himself and that his only hope lay in the grace of God. As we drove along, Steve asked me if we could pray together; and somewhere in the middle of Alabama, Steve's Father in Heaven gave him more than a new pair of shoes—on that day Steve accepted Jesus Christ as his Lord and Savior.

22

Up a Hill

IT WAS the night before the Georgia Tech game. We were staying at the Crowne Plaza Hotel in Atlanta. It had been a long day for the scout team. Tech had a lot of different sets, and our job for three days had been to emulate the array of weaponry in Coach Paul Hewitt's backcourt. B. J. Elder was a force to be reckoned with, one that was tough to duplicate in practice.

I loved the trip to Georgia. It was a quick flight, and Atlanta was always an enjoyable city. One of our players, Chris Ellis, from nearby Marietta, would always say, "You know wassup, Al Will? Nothing like that ATL."

After an eight-hour rest and a trip to the breakfast buffet, the team traveled to the McDonald's Center for our shoot-around. As we entered the arena, I noticed the location of the opposing team's locker room. It was incredibly inconvenient. After changing into our practice gear, we had to walk out the locker room door, take a left, a quick right, and then proceed down a narrow, steep, and *long* hallway. It was basically a giant ramp leading to the Yellow Jackets' court.

While the locker room at the top of this "hill" was oddly placed, it was strategic in that it forced the visiting team to walk up and down a fifty-yard ramp every time they needed access to their dressing room. It was annoying. We must have had to do it four times throughout the course of the night. In the four years I went to Atlanta, I learned that the long hallway was indicative of reality on the road in the ACC. Each road game was truly an uphill battle.

As we warmed up that particular night in the "Thriller Dome," I sensed the hostile environment. We were in the middle of Kentucky Shooting, a drill we always did during warm-ups. For a few laughs, the student section behind our basket had been counting out the number of shots we missed in the drill.

This went on for about thirty seconds, as our team missed seven jumpers in a row from the top of the key. I was a little nervous as I made a V-cut toward the baseline. As I flashed my hands upon moving back toward the three-point line, I knew that I was the crowd's least expected candidate to end the streak, but I did. I was pleased with myself. Even one of the coaches who was often quick to point out my mistakes said, "Good job, Al," as I gave a teammate a fist on my way back to the end of the line. As a walk-on, I had to get excited about the little things.

Road games in the ACC were tough, no matter where you went. On the road, you didn't get the best calls, the fans were ruthless, the rims were tighter, and sometimes you had to walk up a mountain just to get to your locker room.

Thankfully, we won the game that night. While many people left the arena thinking, *Man, that Justin Gray guy can really shoot* (Justin scored 26 points), the teammate with whom I was most impressed was Chris Paul. Chris was a McDonald's All-American from Winston-Salem. Everyone in town loved him—Dick Vitale often referred to him as "the mayor of Winston-Salem." Chris was without a doubt the best freshman point guard in the country. He was good, but he still wanted to be better. He was a leader, a competitor, and a coachable player all at the same time. If you watched Chris's body language on TV, you'd never know that his jump shot was off because all he cared about was winning.

Unlike many players in sports today, Chris knew how to take criticism. He listened to what Coach Prosser said, good or bad, and utilized it to make himself a better player. It was not uncommon to see Chris in the coach's office watching extra film. Not enough players ask the question, "How can I get better, Coach?"

I stretched next to Chris each day, and I'll never forget hearing about a great moment of courage. His grandfather had unexpectedly passed away at the beginning of his senior season in high school. In order to show how much he loved his grandfather, Chris dedicated his next performance to his memory. With minutes remaining in the fourth quarter of his next game, he converted a lay-up and was fouled in the attempt. What would have normally been a routine free throw was anything but, as Chris went to the line and intentionally air-balled the shot. With that, he checked himself out of the game and went over to his dad (an assistant coach) on the bench and hugged him as tightly as he could. Chris scored 61 points that November night. His grandfather was 61 years old when he passed away.

Chris's missing the rim for his grandfather wasn't the last time he ever gave up points. Prior to the Georgia Tech game, we played Cincinnati, and Chris had scored thirty. He was spectacular, and many people might have expected him to hand Georgia Tech's Jarrett Jack the same medicine, but he didn't. That's not what our

---

It's amazing what a group of people can accomplish when nobody cares who gets the credit.

—JOHN WOODEN

---

team needed. That night, Chris took on a passer's mentality and scored only 2 points in a memorable victory.

As the buzzer sounded at the end of the game, we calmly shook our opponent's hands and made our way through the tunnel to the base of the long hallway. From there, many of us began to sprint up the ramp. We were screaming and yelling because we knew that we were the first team that season to have beaten the future Final Four team at home.

As we continued toward the locker room, I can still picture the scene. Everyone was sharing in the victory. The walk-ons were yelling, and better yet Big E was shouting as loud as he could. It didn't matter who it was; we were all pumped up. We had sixteen players on our team; and during the course of that game, some of us had scored 28 points, some of us 2 points, and some of us zero points. We didn't have the same role, but we did have an identical goal. We all wanted a win that night in Atlanta and didn't care who got the credit.

By now, the big ramp didn't seem as steep. As my teammates

and I neared the end of the hallway, I heard Chris Paul say something I will never forget: "That's right, that's right. I'll take two points and a win any day."

And with that, we made our way to the top.

PRESS CONFERENCE
Finishing the Race

Whenever I went home for Christmas, everyone was so encouraging: "We're so proud of you, Alan"; "We watch all of your games on TV." In the midst of this sort of flattery, one night at a Christmas party, one man took a different approach when he looked me square in the eyes and said, "Alan, let me tell you something, son. I've been watching your team and from the looks of things, it doesn't look like you're going to be getting a lot of playing time this year. So, if you can't get P.T., you gotta get C.T. Do you know what C.T. is, Alan?"

"No, sir, what is C.T?"

"Camera Time . . . and if you want more camera time, it's very simple, son. During a time-out, always go high-five the hand of the player who made the last big play. And always stand behind the head coach in the huddles."

It was a turning point in my career. I had been inspired. From that moment on, through hard work and determination, my C.T. increased every year I played.

23

Together

I WAS ALWAYS one of the first guys to the arena because I liked to shoot. If a game was at seven, we had between five and six o'clock to practice on our own. I loved shooting around to the sounds of blaring music in the arena. It made me feel good, and as a player who didn't get much action once the game started, I got up as many shots as I possibly could. I had to get there early if I wanted to shoot, because when the key players arrived, I had been encouraged to put my shooting passion aside.

Coach Prosser always watched the shoot-around, and one day I was busy pouring in threes when he motioned me over to where he was sitting. He got up out of his chair, and as I walked toward him, he motioned me closer as if he had something important to tell me. Coach put his hand on my shoulder and said to me in a semi-serious, yet kidding, voice—otherwise known as sarcasm, "Alan, I've been watching you. Your jumper looks really good right now, and it makes me feel really good sitting over here knowing that if I need you tonight, you're greased and ready to go. But I'm a little more worried about some of these other guys getting up shots. No offense, Alan; your jumper looks good now, but I think you should have more of a passer's mentality in warm-ups from now on."

From that moment on, I got to the arena extra early so that I could shoot on my own. Gradually, as the scholarship guys began to file in, I would become a passer and take Josh Howard through a light shooting workout—*I'd try to lead our team in pre-game assists.*

One night, I was running behind and showed up at Joel Coliseum the same time as all of my other teammates. Keep in mind that Coach had been reminding us to look nice before the games. He said, "I want this team to come into the arena looking like a classy bunch of guys." Coach told us that Michael Jordan always wore a suit before and after every game. We certainly were not expected to wear suits, but we had to look presentable. In an attempt to heed Coach's advice, I showed up wearing a button-down collared shirt and a pair of khaki pants.

Knowing I was behind schedule, I quickly made my way into the dressing room, a square room with lockers all the way around. As I put my wallet and keys in the drawer in front of my stool, I noticed that Taron, who lockered next to me, was staring at my feet. He said, "Al Will, come on, dawg. How you gonna wear them dirty boots to the game?"

"What you talking about, man?"

"Y'all check out Al Will's boots he got on." From a nearby locker, Justin came over to take a look.

"Al Will got them work boots on. He doesn't clean 'em or nothin'. He just wears 'em." Then someone else chimed in, "Look at those scars on them boots, y'all." Then another, "Someone needs to take Buddy to get some Timberlands for real. He gotta do somethin'."

I was wearing a pair of brown leather hiking boots. I had dressed as normally as I possibly could. I knew that my hiking boots were a nice pair of boots—they were supposed to be worked in and definitely looked better with a little character on them. At this point, I looked around and observed what some of the other guys were wearing: Taron was sporting a tilted baseball hat, an extra-large throwback jersey with blue jeans, and perfectly white Air Force One tennis shoes. Justin was sporting similar shoes, but he had gone with a velour suit. Trent was wearing a white long-sleeved t-shirt that stretched all the way down past his knees. Is that what I was supposed to wear?

I guess you could say that this incident was the first of many good-natured wardrobe clashes that I had with my teammates. In four years, I can't believe how many times I heard the words, "Y'all look what Al Will is wearin'. No, he did not." So I didn't have all the "tightest" gear.

During my time at Wake, all of the fraternities on campus had theme parties. One night was "Disco Night," another "Welcome to the Jungle," but I remember one particular theme was "Rap Video Night." Each person that came to the party was required to dress up as a rapper. I had a few basketball clothes I suppose could have been converted into rapper material, but I couldn't seem to put it together. I called Justin Gray.

"Justin, man, I gotta go to a party tonight and dress up. You mind if I borrow some of your clothes?"

"Oh, no problem, man. We'll fix you up. Just stop by my room sometime tonight. If I'm not there, Big E probably will be."

Later that night, I made my way over to the basement of Luter Hall and knocked on Justin's door. Justin was gone, but Eric was intently playing video games. I told Eric the situation, and he gladly contributed to my cause. He outfitted me with some of his gear that he still had from the McDonald's All-American game. After getting a few more side items (a chain and a hat) from J-Gray's side of the closet, I was good to go.

Later that night, I walked into the party wearing a Michael Jordan Washington Bullets throwback jersey, Nike Air Force high-tops, and a New York Knicks hat tipped to the side. I was authentic, dawg!

One of the aspects of my basketball career I appreciated most was the chance to be around players from different places: North Carolina, Michigan, New York, Ohio, Lithuania, and Panama. We liked different kinds of movies. Most of us went to different churches. Some of us liked country and some rap. Some of us wore dirty hiking boots, and some of us wore clean hiking boots.

These differences, however, were meaningless. For our differences were *not* greater than our similarities. We all wanted to win, and we all wore the same jersey—we were teammates. We won together; we lost together. We cared about each other. And when I was looking for a place to eat Thanksgiving lunch my senior year, Chris Paul didn't hesitate. He said, "Be there at one o'clock." His family prayed, ate turkey, and watched the Cowboys—just like my family did. And when we beat Duke, I didn't look for another walk-on; I hugged Big E, the first person I saw.

At one point during my senior year we found ourselves on a three-game losing streak. I'll never forget the players-only meeting we had. We went around the room and discussed problems we had on our team.

Everyone suggested we couldn't recover and that we were done for the season. I told them, "Fellas, it's one thing for other people not to believe in us, but we have no choice. We've got to believe that we can come out of this because we're all we got."

"We're all we got" was right, and at this point Justin Gray gave one of the most moving speeches I've ever heard. He was a captain, and as he began to speak, he started to cry. His words were slow, as he shared how much he loved each one of us and that he

---

Teamwork is the ability to have different thoughts about things; it's the ability to argue and stand up and say loud and strong what you feel. But in the end, it's also the ability to adjust to what is the best for the team.

—TOM LANDRY

---

was willing to do anything for any of us. He said, "I'd give the shirt off my back for any of y'all." He told us that we were going to turn our season around and that he was going to work harder than ever before because he didn't want to let any of us down.

Following that meeting, it was not uncommon for Justin Gray to be the first guy in the gym. He did extra shooting with the coaches and even ran suicides before practice to get in better shape. This was the kind of attitude that took our team to the Sweet Sixteen that year.

My senior year, I remember sitting for pictures for the media guide at the beginning of the preseason. I was the last guy in line, and while I waited, Taron approached me: "Al Will, let me get your keys. I'm gonna start your car. We'll wait on you."

"Here you go." I tossed Taron the keys. I had given a few of the guys a ride over to where we were taking the photos, and they wanted to cool off the car while they waited for me. Three minutes later, I walked outside and one of the guys in the car said, "Get in the back. We're goin for a ride, Al-Weezy." At that moment, six of my teammates were in the car with the stereo blaring rap. There was nowhere for me to sit. As I looked at them with a puzzled look on my face, one of them said to me again, "Get in the back. We going for a ride, Al Will."

I opened the tailgate on my truck, got in, and sat next to my golf clubs and the other clutter in the back. From there, Taron rolled down the windows, and we cruised around Wake Forest. As we circled the campus, my teammates only turned down the music to wave at the pretty girls: "How you doin', ladies?"

That day in the car was one I will never forget. I'm not sure who was singing the music that was playing on the radio, but it didn't matter—I was with my teammates.

24

Leather Chair

I WAS having dinner with my parents at a restaurant in Dallas. With my dad's handheld radio up to my ear, I listened for Josh Howard's name. It was the night of the NBA Draft. As Commissioner David Stern called out the twenty-fifth pick in the draft, I began to get nervous. Josh's name had not been called.

Josh was my teammate for three years at Wake Forest, so I couldn't help but be anxious; even more so when three more picks were revealed without Josh's name being called. By now, all of the teams that Josh had worked out for had passed him up. There was one pick left in the first round. As I heard the commissioner begin to speak, I put my Dr. Pepper down and held my breath, hoping Josh would not slip into the second round.

"With the twenty-ninth pick in the 2003 NBA Draft, the Dallas Mavericks select Josh Howard from Wake Forest University." We were ecstatic. Not only had Josh's name been called, but he was drafted by my favorite team as a little kid. In addition to that, I knew him—he was my teammate.

A week later, Mavericks owner Mark Cuban flew Josh to Dallas to begin summer league play. I was already in Dallas working for a law firm, and Steve Lepore had come to visit that same week. I figured it would be great if we could all hang out, so I called Josh to let him know Steve was in town and that it would be a good time to go see the Texas Rangers, who happened to be playing that night. I thought a baseball game in Arlington would give him a good dose of Texas.

After I made the offer, Josh surprised me with his response. He said, "I think I'm already gonna be there, Buddy."

"That's cool man. Who are you going with, Josh?"

"I dunno. They said a limo's coming to get me in about an hour. I think I'm supposed to throw out the first pitch or something like that."

The only thing better than being close to the field was to be on it, so I guess you could say that Josh definitely didn't need my tickets that night. Although he was a big-timer now, he was still Josh Howard. Upon being introduced, the fans at Ameriquest Field gave him a huge ovation. They were clapping for someone who was going to be a part of their basketball team. I, on the other hand, was clapping for someone whom I knew, someone I respected, and someone who always stood up for me.

Nearly a year and a half before Josh made his Texas debut, our team finished a tough practice at Joel Coliseum. Josh was a junior and I was a sophomore. As the huddle broke, I walked through the tunnel towards our locker room door. It was always a treat to walk into our dressing room. As I walked through the doorway, I passed the pictures on the wall showing all the Wake Forest greats that made it to the NBA—the locker room was first class.

On the center wall were four TV's, three standard size and one large plasma screen. In the middle of the room was a round, wooden table with a WF in the center. In front of the table were two large black leather sofas and a few matching leather chairs (thrones for only the best players). It was here that we had our scouting reports before each game.

The one glitch about our meeting room was that there weren't enough seats on the sofas and chairs for all sixteen players to sit. Consequently, there were three or four stools directly behind the sofas—and this is where I always sat. On days we met, I naturally passed over the sofas and sat on the steel stools.

For whatever reason, this particular day was different. I walked into the locker room, got a Gatorade out of the cooler, and sat down in one of the big leather chairs. It was an ambitious move, but I was tired of sitting on the stools. As I sat down, one of the members of the basketball staff immediately confronted me and said, "Come on, man, let Josh and those guys sit in those chairs."

I was only a sophomore at the time, so I conformingly nodded my head, got up from the seat, and made my way back to my stool. I didn't know it at the time, but Josh Howard happened to be right behind me and had heard my exchange with the coach. He said, "No, Buddy, go back and sit down. You straight—Buddy sitting up there today, Coach. I'll sit on one of the stools back here." The assistant coach, of course, couldn't say anything to Josh. On that day, for the first time, I listened to the scouting report from the big leather chair. Josh made me forget that I was a walk-on.

In reality, Josh Howard probably doesn't even remember doing what he did, but I do. It meant a lot to me. Josh was the star of our team. He played all of the minutes and scored most of the points. Conversely, I was the walk-on who rarely got minutes and hardly ever scored. To this day, whenever I think about Josh Howard, I never think about the fact that he was the ACC Player of the Year or that he was a first-round NBA Draft pick. Instead, I think about the one day that he cared enough to give up his chair for a walk-on like me.

25

A New York Minute
with Dick Vitale

MADISON SQUARE GARDEN is known today as the world's most famous arena. For decades, championship teams and stars have sold out the historic landmark. Whether it was the Rangers winning the Stanley Cup or the Knickerbockers winning the NBA championship, the Garden has seen a lot. In 1970, Joe Frazier beat Muhammad Ali. Later that decade, Elvis Presley sold out four shows. Frank Sinatra dazzled music fans in 1974, the Pope came in 1979, Bruce Springsteen in 1987, Madonna in 1993, and Elton John in 2001.

And then there was me—I came in 2001.

I loved the Garden and am proud to say that I played there four times over the course of my career. Following my first game at the Garden, I received a letter from my grandfather explaining that I was *not* the only family member to play at the historic arena. After serving in World War II, Papa went to college and represented the University of Rochester in the venue that I would warm up in nearly fifty years later.

My most memorable trip to Madison Square Garden came during my final season. It was our first game of the year. We were playing Memphis in the Coaches versus Cancer Charity Classic. As I stepped off our bus to enter the arena, I could feel New York. I smelled vendors' hot dogs, heard honking taxis, and felt the chill of the air. I was in the Big Apple. As a K-9 cop walked past our bags at the security checkpoint, I marveled at the pass which dangled around my neck—it read PARTICIPANT.

While I was in awe of the atmosphere that night, during the shoot-around, I was saddened by the fact that my dad's treatment had prevented him from being at the game. We were playing my old hometown, and as I saw John Calipari's Memphis Tigers at the other end of the floor, I thought about how much my dad would have liked this scene.

He had driven all the way from Texas to approximately half of my games the year before, but now all I could do was look at our parents' section and hurt over his not being there. I suppose the second best thing to actually being at the Garden, though, was to turn the TV to ESPN and watch the game through the eyes of Dick Vitale, who was pacing about the arena as we warmed up.

As I kept shooting, I noticed Dick Vitale and admired his ability to engage with the fans during his preparation for the telecast. He is a legend in college basketball; his energy and stamina on TV are unmatched. I love his catchy one-liners: how he calls coaches who play easy schedules "Cream Puff Delights" and refers to up-and-down players as "Dow Jonesers."

I realized, however, that the man who represents college basketball with so much enthusiasm was the same person who could do me a huge favor. While no one was looking, I took a pad and pen went into the bathroom as the rest of my teammates continued to stretch in the locker room. Here, I sat down and composed a letter to Dick Vitale:

DEAR DICKEY V,

You don't know me, but my name is Alan Williams, and I am #20 for Wake. My Dad's name is Bowman Williams, + he can't be here tonight because he's waiting to begin chemotherapy treatment in Texas. Since he can't be here, I was wondering if you would be willing to say 'hi' to Him during the game + tell him how much I love him + that I wish he could be here.

I also want you to know how much it means to me that you continue to help raise support in the fight for cancer. I've heard your message about the late Nc. St. Coach Jim Valvano many times, + you always remind people like my Dad to "never give up; don't ever give up." I hope you can help me out.

Sincerely,

As the stretching was about to conclude, I could hear "Where's Al Will?" from the other side of the bathroom door, but I had to finish the letter. I knew my teammates were about to huddle up, so I folded the piece of notebook paper, stuffed it in my sock, and joined my teammates for the Lord's Prayer.

After making sure the note was secure one more time, I took the court with my teammates. As I ran by center court, I saw Dan

Shulman and Dickey V doing their pregame analysis in front of the camera. I was nervous. I lacked the courage to hand him the note on the first round of lay-ups. The second time around, though, I saw that he was finished. I rebounded another lay-up and made a bounce pass to one of my teammates as I trotted to the back of the line—directly in front of the broadcasting super-star.

He doesn't want to be bothered right now, I thought. I knew I wasn't going to get in the game, so if I was going to make my move, I had to do it now. As I approached the end of the lay-up line, I extended my stride two extra steps and tapped Dickey V on the shoulder. In an anxious and out of breath voice, I asked him, "Will you read this when you get a chance?"

He looked at me with an inquisitive face and nodded his head. As we proceeded into the Kentucky Shooting drill, I watched out of the corner of my eye and saw the legend unravel the folded note.

An hour later, as I sat on the bench enjoying the stellar play of our team, I wondered if Dickey V would really come through for me. Was he going to help me out? I didn't know at this point, but I did know we were whipping up on Memphis. I didn't get any minutes on the court that night, but it was still enjoyable to watch.

Finally, the game ended. After shaking hands with Coach Calipari and the rest of his team, we walked down a hallway and into our locker room. Coach Prosser was in good spirits as he congratulated our efforts before releasing us to shower and pack up—we always met as a team after each game.

Shortly after, I went over to my locker and reached for my cell phone buried in the side pocket of my black travel bag. As always, I looked to see if anyone had called—there were twenty missed calls. I knew what had happened: Dickey V had come through for my dad. Apparently, as I sat on the bench during a free throw in the second half, the camera zoomed in on me, and Dickey V talked about my dad for nearly a minute. He told my dad that I loved him and said, "This is the real reason why we're here tonight at the Coaches versus Cancer Classic. This is what it's all about, man. Bowman Williams, your son told me to tell you how much he loves you, and I want you to know that you are in our prayers. You're going to fight this thing! As the late Jimmy V said, 'Don't give up; don't ever give up, Bowman.'"

I'll never forget the excitement I had as I called my dad after the game. It was incredible to hear how much it meant to him. He wasn't there that night, but Dickey V made him a part of it.

The next day, I ran into Coach Prosser in the student center. He said, "Al Will, that was a good thing Dickey V did for your dad last night." Dickey V obviously knew the importance of time-outs in college basketball, but he also knew the importance of taking a time-out to encourage people.

Not only did Dick Vitale encourage my father during the game that night, but soon after, he did it again. Three weeks after the Memphis game, I had a package waiting for me in Coach Kelsey's office. I didn't get too many pieces of fan mail, so a package with my name on it was a true novelty. As I picked up the package, I looked in the upper left corner and saw Dick Vitale's name in the return address—I wasn't used to that either. I opened up the package and there was a signed copy of his book, *Living a Dream: Reflections on 25 Years Sitting in the Best Seat in the House.* On the cover in black permanent marker read the words, "To Bowman: Keep fighting. Don't ever give up. Sincerely, Dickey V."

Between the pages of the book was another handwritten note

to my dad encouraging him in his battle with cancer. I waited until Christmas to give my dad these things. As he unwrapped the small present, I could see the smile that stretched across his face as he took his glasses off to take a closer look at the gift he will never forget.

After my dad finished, I took the time to read Dickey V's book and was amazed at where basketball has taken him and, more importantly, where he has taken basketball.

His story is notable, one not confined to the screen of a television set. While many heard Dickey V encourage my dad on national TV that night, nobody saw him reach into his desk weeks later to pull out a small sheet of paper to write my dad a quick note to remind him to "keep fighting." A simple, yet powerful, act like this didn't find a place in Vitale's latest book, but it certainly found a place in my dad's heart.

One day, I got a chance to ask my dad what it was really like to be encouraged by Dickey V on ESPN that November night. He told me, "I have many memories walking alongside you during your basketball career, but that one will always be special."

A month after playing in the Garden, I was warming up in lay-up lines, yet again. Only this time, it was in Cameron Indoor Stadium. We were about to play Duke, and I saw Dickey V pacing about half-court. I walked by him to get his attention, and as I caught his eye, I said, "Thanks." He smiled back—he knew what I was talking about. Like a real time-out in college basketball, the time it took for Dick Vitale to write a short note to my dad was only a minute. But its impact will never be forgotten.

26

11.34 Seconds

AFTER home games, the players always went back out into the arena to visit with friends and family. To get back to the court, we had to walk through a tunnel that was lined with little kids, desperately waving their arms behind the rails in hopes of getting an autograph.

As players, we signed more on the weekends. One Saturday afternoon, as usual, I was the first player to walk out of the locker room—I didn't have to shower after games. As I made my way through the tunnel, the kids, slowly but surely, began to recognize me in my street clothes. It was not uncommon for an eight-year-old to make sure I was legit: "Are you a player, sir?" I always said graciously, "Yes, I am." Even though I wasn't the prototype D-1 basketball player, they still wanted my autograph. That particular day, they all waved their pens in my direction.

"Hey, will you sign this? Will you sign this?"

"Can you sign my arm, please, sir?"

"No problem," I said as I wondered how much my autograph

was actually worth. By now, I had twenty kids reaching their hands down from the stands waiting for me to sign my name. I loved it; if you were to look back at some of my old textbooks from junior high, you would see most of my pages filled with my "practice" autographs. This was the real thing though; and just as I was putting my signature on a little redhead's poster, I heard a scream: "There's Josh Howard!" Before I could sign "Williams," the kid jerked the Sharpie out of my hand and, along with all of the other kids, rushed over to where Josh was.

Being a walk-on was definitely humbling in many ways. The bottom line was that we were not the most recognizable guys on the team. We didn't have a glamorous role. In four years, the amount of playing time I received never changed. It was a long road, but I can honestly say that during my senior year, things were different. Why? Because I finally had a fancy picture above my locker—the masking tape from freshman year was gone. No longer was I the brunt of dinner table jokes. I had all the gear, my jersey fit perfectly, and I even got my own page in the media guide, a picture and all.

At the beginning of the season that year, we voted for team captains. Shortly after the voting, Coach Battle came up to me and asked, "Al Will, come on, man. You voted for yourself, didn't you?"

"No, Coach, I promise I didn't. I voted for Justin, Taron, and Lev."

"Really? Well you got two or three votes. That's not bad, Al Will."

I didn't get elected captain that year, but knowing that I had received a few votes reminded me that my role on the team had changed. In my own way, I was a leader now; I was the only senior on the team, and the guys showed me respect. My teammates stopped by my apartment all the time to hang out. T-Bug and

Critty loved my slice 'n' bake cookies—that's all I could make. When Kyle had a surprise birthday party, I was in charge.

Before conditioning on the track one day, one of the freshmen came up to me and said, "How bad is it going to be today? I don't know if I can make it, Al Will." I was now the one assuring the younger guys that they would make it. When another freshman threw up after our first day of running, I was able to tell him, "Hey, man, you're good. The same thing happened to me the first time I conditioned. Don't sweat it, big fella." In four years, I went from wearing a coat and tie in the team picture to holding the ball in the front row—times had changed.

I had been around. I was by no means the captain of our team, but coach still allowed me to lead. Coach Prosser referred to me as the "Captain of the Walk-ons." In my senior year, we had three other walk-ons, and my role was no more important than theirs.

We played hard as a scout team—it was our job to get the starters ready to play. Everyday, we arrived at practice thirty minutes early to learn the other team's offense. Within a two-day period, we'd often learn up to fifteen sets. Some of our other responsibilities in practice included passing to other players while they did their shooting drills. It wasn't until my senior year that I participated in this part of practice. It was not uncommon to walk in and see one of us holding a yellow pad playing "dummy defense" in a drill. Sometimes we'd stay on defense for thirty minutes.

As a scout team, our favorite moments came when we ran our opponent's offensive sets against the first team. In the end, we did whatever was necessary to make our team more prepared. And Coach didn't forget about our role. After a big win, he'd often say, "Great win, fellas. Scout guys, you got us ready—good work."

What made our scout team so effective my senior year was that we all meshed together. The four walk-ons genuinely wanted each other to do well, and together, we took great pride in our roles on the team.

As a scout team we got excited about little things. We got fired up when Richard had a dunk or when Scotty Benken took a charge. And how could you not get pumped after Scott Feather ripped Chris Paul or when Johnny Buck nailed a baseline jumper. There was no better feeling than to beat the starters in a practice clip and know these were the same guys that were going to win an ACC game the next day.

While most of the scout team's action came in practice, there were times when our walk-on efforts were rewarded. These rewards usually came at the end of a game during a blowout. I don't think Coach Prosser liked it when the fans screamed, "We want Alan," but I'll never forget the time I got in the last two minutes against Elon. In the shoot-around hours before the game, I was practicing a move I had done a number of times in high school—a double-behind-the-back crossover. Condescendingly, my teammates and coaches told me there was no way I would ever use the move in a game and that it was only effective against *no defense*.

Needless to say, the time was ticking away at the end of the Elon game—we were up thirty points and "scrub time" was going by fast. With thirty seconds left on the clock, it was always customary for Coach to give the *no more shots* signal. This meant we were supposed to let the clock run down out of respect to the other team. The thoughtfulness demonstrated class and good sportsmanship, but it limited walk-on shot attempts.

Anyhow, with fifteen seconds to go in the game, we were playing defense when a long rebound came off the rim. I grabbed it and took off for our basket at the other end. With the ball in hand, I looked straight ahead, intentionally cutting off all communication with Coach Prosser. He may have been yelling to slow it down, but I had a one-track mind.

Nearing the three-point line, I made my way down the right side of the floor. An Elon player was directly in front of me; he was backpedaling, and one of his teammates was running along beside me to my left. Everyone else was bringing up the rear behind me. As it came time to make a move on my defender, I thought, *Do the move, do the move. Do it, Alan.*

I had already hit a three a minute before this, so my confidence was high. I had to do it. This was my only chance. As I passed the three-point line, I crossed over behind my back to my left hand and then back to my right—all in one motion. As expected, both of my defenders lunged to the left, paving the way for a right-handed finger roll.

After looking behind me to make sure it went in, I ran toward our bench, pointing at all of my teammates as I went by, "I told you I'd do it, I told you." My teammates and the rest of the arena loved it. I'm not sure what Coach Prosser thought, but I'm sure he was smiling on the inside. To this day, I've convinced myself that the move would have been a *SportsCenter* top-ten play had the game been televised. Maybe not, but I did make the local news that night. The next week Dave Goren, a sports anchor in Winston, did a special feature on me and coined my *infamous* move: *The Shot Heard around the World.* It's amazing what you have to do to get a little press these days.

It was never easy sitting on the bench for two hours and then getting your name called to check into the game, but as walk-ons, we gratefully took advantage of the opportunities we were given. If we played, that was great; but if not, we were going to be the most encouraging and noisy bench in the ACC.

One of my greatest memories at Wake came on a road trip to Dallas. I had lived there until I was twelve, so I was reminiscent as I shot around in Moody Coliseum. The gym still smelled the same as it did when I shot there as a kid. Dad, my brother Campbell, and I always played a game of H-O-R-S-E whenever we found a door that was open.

Now, I was warming up with Wake Forest. As I did, the head coach of SMU came to shake my hand and wish me good luck. Both of my grandparents, my cousins, little-league coaches, parents' friends, college friends, and other people whom I recognized were in attendance.

More than ever, I wanted to get on the floor that night. If we had home court advantage, I would have projected some playing time (it was a walk-on tradition to predict possible playing time), but I knew the Ponies were tough at home and would take advantage of the momentum they had after beating a tough Bobby Knight team only a few days before.

I was right—the game was tight. With only five minutes to go, it was a two-possession game. As the clock ticked down to the one-minute mark, we hit two free throws to extend our lead, now 8 points. By now, getting to play was out of the question; Coach Prosser never put walk-ons in without at least a 20-point lead.

Unexpectedly, though, with about 30 seconds left on the scoreboard, a group of people in the stands began to start the familiar cheer from back home in Winston-Salem: "Alan Williams—*clap,*

clap—Alan Williams." Since Moody Coliseum was a small arena, everyone could hear it. Seconds later, others began to catch on. More people began to yell, "Put him in, Coach. Give him a chance—this is his hometown." Let me be very clear, this was not like the movie *Rudy*. Nobody was crying—nobody had the chills—everyone just thought it would be really funny if I got in the game.

I was embarrassed as I sat in my seat because I knew Coach Prosser wouldn't crack. A road game like this was too important for seeding in the NCAA Tournament to mess around with crowd demands. With about 20 seconds to go, one of our players went to the free throw line again. By now, Coach's approval rating was sinking as fans behind the bench continued to urge the coach to put me in.

Coach had his hands in his pockets and was now pacing back and forth across the sideline—he was furious. His face was red, and his teeth were clenched as he held up his fingers in the air to call the defense. On the other hand, I was smiling because it wasn't my fault the crowd didn't know the *20-point rule*. Once again, there was a foul—more time for deliberation. With 11.34 seconds, we were up 8 points. Coach's conscience was killing him; he had to do something.

He turned directly around to where the four assistant coaches were sitting, put his finger in their faces, and said something most memorable, "Is there anything Alan Williams can do in ten seconds to lose this game?" I'm not sure what their answer was, but within a fraction of a second, I saw Coach Prosser point in my direction: "Al Will."

The fans were going wild. I could see Coach Prosser swallow deeply as he saw my un-Division-One-like body take off my warm-ups and run toward him. He put his hand on my shoulder and gave me a few last-second instructions: "Don't shoot and don't foul."

"Now checking into the game, number twenty, Alan Williams."

I could hear the roar of the crowd. I was in the game now. As I started to trot down to the action, I was halted by Coach Prosser, "Alan, just stay here. Why don't you go to the corner." If I were a coach, I probably would have said the same thing. "Coach" Chris Paul told me otherwise, though. He yelled at me from the free throw line and signaled that he was going to get me the ball. I could see the urgency in his face—he wanted to get me a basket. I figured if anyone could get me a bucket, Chris could.

Unfortunately, SMU fouled again, forcing one of my teammates to go to the line. During the free throw, I geared up for defense. After the shot was released, I backpedaled down the court where I did my best to deny my man the basketball. Surprisingly, the SMU player to my right started to fumble the ball as he dribbled. I saw the ball rolling on the ground, so I dived. As I did, the man I was guarding cut me off in the air. We both went down, the whistle blew, and a foul was called on #20—me. I thought it was good hustle, but the referee didn't. And neither did Coach Prosser as he pointed to his head as if to say, *THINK!*

By now there were 8 seconds left. As one of the SMU players took a shot from the weak side, I crashed the boards and grabbed the long rebound. I thought about holding the ball for the last 6 seconds, but I figured that wouldn't make for a very good ending. So, I took off with the ball. I took two hard dribbles with my right hand, crossed over to my left like Jimmy Chitwood in *Hoosiers*, and let a bomb go from half-court. It was nothing but backboard, and the game ended. No one carried me off the court. Despite the hard miss, the crowd loved it. I mean, how many times have you seen the winning team take an unnecessary half-court shot?

I celebrated the win with my family after the game for a few short moments and then got on the team bus. Thirty minutes later, we pulled up beside our plane at Love Field. I was the second-to-last guy to get off the bus. I could see Coach Prosser still looking at his stat sheet at the front. I didn't know if I should say anything, but I did: "Coach, I just wanted to say thanks for putting me in. That meant a lot to me to be able to play in front of my family and friends. I know you didn't have to do that. Thanks."

He looked up to listen to what I had to say and nodded his head. As I was about to get off the bus he finally spoke to me: "Dumb foul."

Coach putting me in the game had said enough, so I brushed off the foul comment and took my seat on the plane. Besides, everyone thought I played well. As my dad likes to say, I had a "triple"—a foul, a rebound, and a half-court shot—all in a matter of seconds!

During my career, I found that I didn't always "get in the game" as much as I wanted. However, I learned that whether I was sitting on the end of the bench or heaving half-court shots, I had to give it my all. Sometimes in life, you only get 11.34 seconds—make the most of it.

THE MORNING PAPER
Reflections

I was thirteen years old. We were on our way home from an AAU tournament. All the doors were locked, but one. Thankfully, my little brother, Bo, had found a newspaper stuck in one of the side doors of the Dean Dome. Minutes later, I marveled as I shot around amid the sea of blue. My dad took pictures of me as I dribbled around the shiny court, all the while staring at the #23 jersey in the rafters. I dreamed of one day playing in the ACC.

As a senior in college, I came back to Chapel Hill for the fifth time. I had no trouble getting in. After our shoot-around was over, I asked one of my teammates to take a picture of me on the court. Coach said, "Hey, Al Will, this isn't the senior class trip. Let's go." It had been nine years since my first trip to the Dean Dome. I was twenty-two years old. I had been playing in the ACC for almost four years. I was still dreaming about it.

27

Different Doors

TODAY IS May 10, 2004, and I just left the men's basketball locker room. I had to clean out my locker. The season has been over for a couple months now; and I needed to clear out my belongings, so that one of the incoming freshmen could take over my spot this summer.

I tried to keep it as long as I could, but today I took my final exams. Unfortunately, this is all I had left to do. A few minutes ago, I punched in my four-digit code, heard the click, and entered our players' lounge. As I walked inside the familiar room, the lights came on, and I began rummaging through the closet to see if I could find a box to put all of my gear in. I couldn't find one, so I settled for a clear trash bag.

Soon after, I walked back into the lounge and passed the two black leather sofas where we used to watch tape.

With my plastic bag in hand, I walked over to my locker, the first one on the right. I pulled up a garbage can; I had lots of gum wrappers to throw away. In the bottom of my locker, I picked up two green Gatorade water bottles with my number on them. They were still half full of water. In one corner, there were several loose socks without a match.

After getting rid of what I didn't need, I proceeded to sort through the fifteen pairs of Nike shoes that sat on the wooden shelves. As I glanced over the shoes, I was reminded of how I had earned that gear, and that it wasn't always there. My running shoes were on the bottom shelf; they made me think of the painful hours I spent touching lines and trying to make suicide times. I remembered the feeling I would have in my stomach when coach would say, "All of you better make it or you're all going again."

The sandals I sometimes wore in the shower reminded me of the sense of accomplishment that I always had after workouts. Some of the shoes on the top right shelf were the ones I wore when we went on road trips. I thought about how I would miss laughing at the back of chartered planes, sitting next to Chris and Vytas on the bus, and shooting around in opposing teams' arenas. Each pair had its own memory. One pair I wore when we beat Duke—twice we beat the Blue Devils—and I can still see the scowl on Mike Krzyzewski's face as I passed him on the way to the bus after those games. In another pair, we clinched Wake Forest's first regular season ACC Title since 1964. And I couldn't forget the shoes I wore in the Sweet Sixteen.

While my game shoes were barely worn, my practice shoes were scuffed up and scattered throughout the middle shelf. How I survived four years of practice I don't know, but I do know that I will miss it—the shooting clips, the two-on-one fastbreak drills, and even the "perfection drill."

At last, there were the shoes I wore in the senior game in April with Chris Duhon and other ACC seniors. My favorite moment of that game was watching my man go screen Chris, and then instructing the Duke star what to do: "Chris! Switch. You got mine, you got mine." I was not able to do that very much. And surprisingly, I beat the All-American point guard to win the three-point shootout. Unlike Chris, though, I wasn't entering the NBA Draft.

As I put the last pair of shoes in the bag, I noticed the sheet of paper that was taped to my locker. It was a sheet of paper with a picture of the Alamo Dome to remind us that, during the season, our ultimate goal was to make the Final Four in San Antonio. As I took the piece of paper down, I looked at the right wall of my locker where there was a picture of my dad, one of my favorite quotes, and a Bible verse from Philippians that talked about "finishing the race."

It served as a reminder that this particular race had come to a close. By now, I had placed my last belongings in the sack. Before walking out of this room, I looked around and saw the other players' lockers. They were still filled with plenty of Nikes and practice gear. As for me, my locker was now empty. All that was there was the picture that hung directly above my locker—a giant superimposed picture of me surrounded by a series of fancy graphics. On the top, was my name and number. Each player had one.

I stared at the picture, realizing that sixteen years of dedication and hard work had neared its end. As I stared even longer, an appreciation for what I had experienced playing basketball filled my heart like never before.

A few weeks earlier, I had been asked to give my senior remarks at our end-of-the-year banquet before a crowd of nearly 500 people. Coach Prosser stood to introduce me and said, "Soon after I arrived at Wake Forest, I received a phone call from Howard Garfinkle, the owner of Five-Star Basketball Camp, and he says to me, 'Skip, congrats on the new job . . . but you gotta make sure you do one thing for me.' And so I say, 'What's that, Garf?' He said, 'You gotta keep Alan Williams on the team.' So then I say, 'What's in Alan Williams?' He says back to me, 'Just keep him on the team. Trust me on this one Skip; you'll never regret it.'"

Coach Prosser admitted that Garf was right. As Coach said

these words, I sat humbly in my chair behind the podium and recalled a few of the conversations my dad and I had when my spot on the team was in question. Dad would always say to me, "Alan, you never know who's going to go to bat for you during this whole process. You never know when someone might put in a good word to Coach Prosser."

After the banquet was over that night, I looked at my father and said, "Hey Dad, I guess we know who went to bat for me now."

I knew Garf followed through in the beginning, but I never knew he had followed through even to the end. He never had to make that phone call, but he did: Garf got me to Wake Forest and made sure I stayed there.

At this point, I made my way out of the lounge door. I walked down the hallway. Along the way, I passed all of the framed jerseys of the greatest players to ever wear the uniform I once wore. My steps were slower than usual. As I passed the last frame, I was confident my jersey would never make it up on that wall.

I knew the next year I would attend a Wake Forest basketball game. On that day, I would enter the coliseum through different doors—I wouldn't have a participant pass. If I stopped by the locker room, I would not be surprised if the code to get in will have changed. And I would not be shocked to see a new face hanging over the locker in the corner. You see, players come and go— that's the way it is.

I turned and looked back for a second. With my gear hoisted over my shoulder, I used my forearm to push the double doors open. I walked away with a lot more than a bag full of shoes.

28

Teammates Matter.

IN FOUR YEARS at Wake Forest, I spent four thousand hours playing basketball. My experience wasn't dependent on any statistic, though. During my career, I played 59 minutes and scored 28 points—*I know what you are thinking, I should have played more.* But in 120 games, I saw the ball go through the net only 10 times.

At the beginning of my story, I made reference to a reporter from the *Greensboro News and Record.* He reminded me during an interview that not many walk-ons survive four years and then he asked why this whole experience was worth it. "What kept you coming back?" he asked.

I told the reporter, "Of course it was worth it." I explained that I had a chance to go to one of the best schools in the country and was able to be a part of college basketball at its best. In four seasons I saw the ACC from the best seat in the house, traveled to every road game, and even had four NCAA Tournament watches and a regular season ACC Championship ring. Despite my unimpressive stat line, it had been an unbelievable experience.

As time has passed, I realize that I had only given the reporter half of the answer to his question that day. While rings and watches and the rest of what I told him were aspects of my experience

I would always be proud of, the lessons learned throughout my career were far more valuable.

Sitting on the end of the bench made me realize that, at different points in our lives, we're all walk-ons. Maybe at times we all feel like we're sitting on the end of the bench. Sometimes we score, and sometimes our shots get swatted to the ceiling. In life, we don't always feel like we can jump as high as the person next to us. We don't always get all of the gear, and it seems like our positions are never guaranteed.

As I continue to look back, I realize that the things the Lord taught me along my journey were a testament to the fact that playing basketball at Wake Forest University was a rewarding experience. To this day, I can't remember the final score of any game. I don't remember what play we ran to beat Duke. And I can't tell you what our field-goal percentage was against Maryland. I don't even remember what our record was. But I do remember the Robert O'Kelleys. I remember the day our best player had enough humility to give up his travel bag to a discouraged teammate. In my closet at home, I now have three of my very own Wake Forest travel bags—all labeled with my name and number. But to this day, whenever I travel, I only use one bag— the bag that bears Robert's #4. It is a continual reminder to me of what it means to be a teammate.

You see, basketball is about a lot more than numbers. I found this to be true on March 22, 2004, because it was on that day that I could finally answer the reporter's question, "What were you fighting for all those years, Alan?"

I was in East Rutherford, New Jersey. We had beaten Virginia Commonwealth and Manhattan in the first and second rounds of the NCAA Tournament. We were facing off against an inspired St.

Joseph's team. That day was one that marked the beginning of change in Wake Forest Basketball. Although we were one of the youngest teams in the field of sixty-five, Coach Prosser had led our team to the Sweet 16 for the first time since the Tim Duncan era. The program was back. However, while this day could only encourage Deacon fans, it marked the end of my career.

A couple of tough guards, Jameer Nelson and Delonte West, had gotten the best of us that night. As I walked along the blue carpet that led to our locker room, I realized my 'hoop dreams' had ended. I began to think about the conditioning, the practices, and all of the hard work that had come before that moment. Now, I was about to take off my jersey for the very last time. In my mind I knew this would be the hardest thing, but I was wrong.

It wasn't. The hardest part came after Coach Prosser finished his post game talk. When he said the words, "Everybody up." This meant that we we were about to huddle up. As I got ready to put my hand in the huddle that day, I looked into the eyes of each of my teammates. I could hear nothing. Though silence prevailed over that small locker room, I could feel everything. I had not played one second that night; but as I looked at my different teammates in the huddle, I could feel Taron's frustrations. I could feel Big E's sweat. And I could feel Justin's tears. It was as if my teammates and I had one single heartbeat, and in the midst of one of the saddest moments of my life, I realized this was what it was all about.

This was why *it was all worth it* and what I would miss the most. I would miss the huddle after painfully going through conditioning. I would miss looking in the eyes of each of my teammates and knowing that whatever we were about to do, we were going to do it together. And most of all, I would miss the feeling of knowing that I was just a small part of a really big thing.

As I put my hands on the shoulders of my teammates, it felt like we would never get over this night. Little did we know, our team had yet to experience true loss. Nobody knew that nearly three years after this huddle would break, all but one of us would gather together in North Carolina, not to celebrate what we had accomplished over the years, but what we would lose. At the age of 54, Coach Prosser, who taught us so much more than basketball, would leave us too early—crying with my teammates in the pews at his funeral would make our St. Joseph's defeat seem small.

As my career ended that night in a quiet locker room, I saw just how much teammates matter. And in that moment, I could now answer that reporter's question, "What were you fighting for all those years, Alan?"

It was the huddle. Getting to stand in a huddle each day with my teammates and coaches—a simple, yet powerful reminder that I was fighting for something greater than self.

With that, I put my hand in the center and, one last time, Coach Prosser said those words, "1…2…3…TEAM!"

In memory of Coach Skip Prosser (1950–2007)

I suppose one can always recruit another player to score points or hire another coach to win games—we can do this because jobs and positions are replaceable. But people—their stories, their character, and their love—are not.

Coach reminded us all that the true treasure of our sports experience would always lie in memories of teammates and coaches: pain we once felt, fears we overcame, laughter we could not suppress, and happiness we could not explain. No picture would ever be clear enough and no trophy shiny enough to capture the joy and the lasting impact of having relationships and being a member of a TEAM.

Epilogue

Teammates Matter is a testament to the fact that much of my college experience relied on the support of my teammates. I could never have imagined making it through my freshman year at Wake Forest without Robert O'Kelley beside me—he taught me how to be a teammate. Robert's professional basketball career ended a few years ago when he was diagnosed with a heart condition. He now lives in Memphis, TN where he is the recreation director at my old church.

Steve was my best friend on the team. We played way too much golf together—I think he beat me once. To this day, Steve Lepore's friendship serves as the biggest reminder of why I was supposed to play college basketball at Wake Forest. After playing in Brighton, England for one season, Steve moved back to Cleveland where he is a sales rep for a major athletic supplier. He still loves the game and stays in much better shape than I do.

After graduating from Wake, I had an opportunity to watch Josh Howard play against Kobe Bryant and the Lakers at the

American Airlines Center in Dallas. I caught his attention in warm-ups. That's when he began waving his hand in the air, "Buddy, Buddy." He even nudged Michael Finley behind him to tell him that was his teammate. I don't know if Mike was interested, but Josh was all smiles because he knew someone in the arena knew exactly where he had come from. Josh Howard continues to be a rising star in the NBA.

Chris Paul left Wake Forest for the NBA Draft after his sophomore season. The next year, he was named NBA Rookie of the Year and shortly after that, helped Team USA reclaim the Gold Medal in the 2008 Summer Olympics.

The only people that can truly understand what a walk-on goes through are walk-ons. I played with eight different walk-ons over my career, but the seasons I spent with Scotty Benken, Johnny Buck, and Scott Feather are most memorable. While each one has his own story, we were a unit, and playing beside them was a privilege. Johnny is now a high school basketball coach in New York, Scott Benken went to pharmaceutical school, and Scott Feather attended law school.

Over the past several years, my father has been in and out of remission. He continues to get his treatments from the trusted doctors at M.D. Anderson Cancer Center in Houston, Texas. Initially, he was one of eleven people that underwent an experimental treatment for his type of cancer. Today, the only member of that group to be declared in complete remission is my dad.

As for me, my hoop dreams are over. It's been almost five years since I played my last collegiate game. Three years ago, I was sharing my story at a luncheon when a mother came up to me afterwards to express her concern for the lack of perspective in sports throughout her community. Perhaps it was that conversation that inspired me to start *Teammates Matter*—a program dedicated to challenging athletes to be the kind of teammates their team-mates need them to be. To date, *Teammates Matter* programs have reached over 200,000 athletes and parents in seventeen states.

Not long after I graduated from Wake Forest, I showed up to a local gym where I was introduced as the assistant coach to a twelve-year old competitive basketball team. In his introduction, the head coach made a concerted effort to brag on me, telling the group of sixth graders how lucky they were to be coached by such a *good* player. About this time, one of the little kids standing in the front row raised his hand, cutting the head coach's introduction short. With a cracked voice, the little kid looked in my direction and said, "Weren't you a benchwarmer?"

I suppose that many aspects of being a walk-on will always be humbling and humorous, but I was still on the team. I will remember my four years at the end of the bench as one of the greatest adventures of my life.

Thanks to all my teammates who made my adventure what it was: Raf, Shoe, Rob, Darius, Erv, C.D., Broderick, Twan, J-Ho, Matt, A.W., Steve, Shetzy, T-Dazzle, JLev, Vytas, Walt, TJ, Brett, R.D., J-Gray, Big E, JI, T-Strick, K-Vis, Todd, Critty, Rich, Johnny, Feather, Benken, C.P., and Scotty P.

2003–2004 Wake Forest Deacons.

Top row, left to right: Greg Collins, Coach Jeff Battle, Coach Skip Prosser, Scott Benken, Jamaal Levy, Eric Williams, Kyle Visser, Vytas Danelius, Todd Hendley, John Buck, Chris Ellis, Coach Chris Mack, Coach Dino Gaudio, Coach Pat Kelsey. *Bottom row, left to right*: Trent Strickland, Scott Feather, Jeremy Ingram, Taron Downey, Alan Williams, Chris Paul, Justin Gray, Richard Joyce

Acknowledgments

I never had a fancy office to write in—just the desk beside my bed at school. In the corner of my room, there were two dry erase boards and a computer. Hanging on my wall were all the chapters of the book, a few pictures of my team, and two sheets of paper that frequently caught my attention. The papers were special because they contained the first notes of my experiences—a bunch of messy handwriting that somehow became *Walk-On: Life from the End of the Bench*. These rough outlines always reminded me that a book doesn't happen overnight. It was a long process and had God not crossed my path with many of the people He did, *Walk-On* & *Teammates Matter* would have remained dreams.

There were plenty of days when I felt like I couldn't keep writing. I am a person who likes to see the end result, and how could I in the midst of such a long project? And what if people didn't like it, what if I never got published, what if *Teammates Matter* was a failure? The "what ifs", however, were overshadowed by a number of people the Lord used to encourage me along the way.

I love Winston-Salem and over the course of four years, I witnessed the fans at Joel Coliseum take their energy to a new level—home court advantage became a tremendous factor. In addition, I know there were many games where our fans saw a twenty-five point lead on our scoreboard, with just a few minutes left in the game. You knew it was over and you could have gone to your cars, but you stayed to the end—thanks.

Wake Forest University is one of the best combinations of basketball and academics in the country. I was blessed to have had an opportunity to be in a challenging learning environment and play the game I love. While this book reiterates that I was not the star, I can honestly say the students and faculty embraced me as if I was.

Dave Odom coached me my freshman year of college. I would have never played basketball for Wake Forest if not for him. I will always be grateful he gave me my start.

Jeff Battle, one of Coach Prosser's assistants, helped me overcome the challenges of being a walk-on. It might have been looking like a rough day for #20, but a raised fist and a smile from Coach B was always an encouragement. I look forward to seeing where he ends up as a head coach. Dino Gaudio had a unique ability to motivate players and I will miss witnessing his passion for the game. Chris Mack was a prime example of how an athlete or coach should compete. Pat Kelsey showed me how a person should approach their job and always made sure I was treated like a scholarship player.

When Coach Prosser arrived, I had two pairs of shoes in my locker, but within a year I had ten. The shoes were not important, but what they symbolized was. I heard a lecture at Five-Star Basketball Camp by Tom Konchalski of HSBI Report. His topic was recruiting and he said, "If you want to know what the head coach is all about, don't ask the star of the team . . . ask the guy that sits at the end of the bench who doesn't get to play. He will tell you what he's really like." Well, I'm that guy and I can attest there is something special about Skip Prosser. Although being a walk-on was tough, I would do it again if I could play for Coach Prosser.

Ron Wellman has taken Wake Forest Athletics to new heights and his encouragement was always appreciated. Dr. Charles Kimball, a well-known professor in the religion department at Wake Forest has been published a number of times. I will never forget scoring against Kansas and how great I felt when he showed a video clip of my basket the next day in class. I continue to be grateful for his advice.

Dr. David Martin, our faithful team doctor, took care of all of us—his enthusiasm and love for the Deacs never went unnoticed. Greg Collins, our trainer, has a demanding job and I am thankful for the way in which he took a genuine interest in our teams. Craig Zakrzewski made sure I always had the same gear as everyone else—I couldn't help but be excited when he returned to Wake my junior year.

Over four years, I learned that more goes into practicing and traveling than meets the eye. Veronica Pagel, Jackie Harris, Chris Jensen, and Tom Norton were managers during my career who poured as much time into the program as the players. Jane Caldwell made sure I stayed on top of my school work. Her job is not easy, but Wake's graduation rate reflects her diligence and concern for academic progress. Julie Griffin loves Wake Forest more than anyone and should write her own book about the Deacs. I will miss her lasagna and her contagious enthusiasm. Jerry Haas let me be a part of the golf team on the range a few times and was always a great fan. Lynne Heflin and Mary Anne Justus made going to the basketball office fun. I always appreciated Dean Buchan's consistency as a person, and Stan Cotton continues to be a fixture in the Wake Forest community and someone I really respect. Special thanks to the Deacon Club for the way in which they enhance the student-athlete experience. The morning paper wouldn't be the same without Dan Collins, and how could I forget "Jim at the Gym," the security guard who used to open Reynolds at night so I could shoot.

Lee Smith was my high school coach and I never loved basketball more than when I played for him. He prepared me for the mental toughness required to play at the next level. He taught me so much more than just the game of basketball.

Eric Sullivan, Ashley Clayton, David Kizer, Jerry Pierce, Eric Harris, Jimmy Seay and Don McConnel also impacted my basketball career and were responsible for teaching me the game.

Several teachers from high school influenced my life, but Mrs. McKinney and Mrs. Nowicki took a special interest in me that extended way beyond Spanish or Algebra II. I wish other students could have an opportunity to have teachers with their commitment.

People often ask me why I coach the Nashville Celtics, my 15 and under summer basketball team. I always tell them that I coach because I have the opportunity to impact young kids' like Dr. Van Snider, my coach, encouraged and influenced my life when I was thirteen. To this day, I still use some of the stories from the devotions he shared with us on road trips. Playing for him made me want to see kids get excited about putting on a new uniform, learning about sportsmanship, and discovering that only Jesus Christ can provide fulfillment in their lives.

Who would have thought my dad's junior high basketball coach would play such an instrumental role in my life? Coach Kellis White's wisdom and unexpected phone calls were always taken to heart.

Howard Garfinkle has done so much for the game of basketball. I was no blue chip, but Garf treated me as if I was. If anyone leaves the game better than when they found it, it will be Garf.

Steve Green helped get me started as one of the first to review my manuscript. As Max Lucado's literary agent, Steve has been a part of many bestsellers. I will always appreciate his willingness to eat breakfast with me and advise an aspiring first time author.

Mike Lewis's encouragement and thoughtful suggestions during the publishing process were especially helpful. I will always be grateful for having the opportunity to work for his firm.

I remember how excited I was to call my former AP English teacher to inform him of the project. The phone call with Dr. Pat Williams turned into a hundred more phone calls. I am thankful my senior year of high school was not the last time he marked up my papers.

Extra thanks to Della Mancuso, Darlene Smith, Laura Deleot, Rudy Wu, Trey Cherry, Courtney Dillard, and Brooke Van Dusen —this project would have never hit the press without your careful attention and hard work.

At Wake Forest, I constantly was surrounded by friends who supported me. Stephen Riddick, Boone Smith, Fred Stone, and Buck Williams—were my golfing buddies who introduced the "We want Alan" chant. Cortland Lowe, Allen Hobbs and Ryan Brown were my roommates freshman year and instilled confidence when my position on the team was far from secure. Mike Scott's selflessness showed me what it means to serve other people. David Sansing's and Blake Schwarz's loyalty will always be remembered. Matt Avery's friendship is a constant reminder of God's faithfulness and I can still remember Stephen Perkins and Phillip Simson rebounding for me before I tried out for the team—only friends do that.

Robbie Anderson, Tucker Davis, and Andy York are three friends from Memphis who knew me long before my walk-on days at Wake Forest. I have many great memories of high school and I continue to value their friendship.

I saw Bill Haas make his first birdie on the PGA tour when he was a sophomore. We were roommates for two years and when I told him I was going to write a book, he answered, "Go write it, man; I want the first copy." Bill never questioned what I was doing.

Kevin Teasley was my R.U.F. campus minister, mentor and close friend. I continue to give thanks for his prayers and wise counsel, never failing to point me to the Lord. I'm certain he will remain a life-long friend.

Scott Abbott, then a member of the SMU golf team, was one of my first teammates. I appreciate Scott's interest in my book—he read more chapters than anyone.

A special thanks to Josh Holden and his family who allowed me to housesit one summer giving me a quiet place to write without distractions. Josh was one of the few who saw this project from beginning to end. He is a great listener and his advice and friendship will always mean a lot.

John Ames, my uncle, was a part of this project from the beginning. Uncle John always did whatever he could to help me. Aunt

Sara has always been an encourager in my life and my cousins, Shelby and Claire, continue to be the sisters I never had.

Mary and Alan Roberts are my grandparents from Fort Worth and have been a blessing in my life. Mimi is full of energy and enthusiasm and I appreciate the character of Abadaddy who I am named after—his humble spirit I certainly admire.

I am also blessed to have Jim Williams as my grandfather. The way he loved my Nana, while she had Parkinson's, was inspiring. He continues to remind me that God's hand is in everything.

I can't forget my sisters-in-law who I love. Mary Gwen's listening ear and caring nature make her special and Betsy's determined spirit and unpredictable humor keep me on my toes. T-Boy, my new *brother*, will never outshoot me, but his approachable personality and his acceptance of me into his family makes him someone I will enjoy being around for a long time to come—and he loves golf.

Mr. and Mrs. Lynch I cannot thank enough—I get to be married to their daughter who they love so well. Their wisdom and understanding for what is important is something I will always respect. They are truly special people and make Brookhaven a place I want to visit often.

We were shooting in the gym my senior year of high school—Dad, Little Bo, and me. Before leaving the gymnasium, Bowman stood at half-court and before shooting the ball, he exclaimed, "If I make this, Alan's going to play basketball for Wake Forest." He did! Little Bo is not so little anymore; he insists he is the strongest of the three of us. The way in which he loves Mom, Dad, Cam, and me is a constant reminder of what family is all about.

Many have said you always want to be like your older brother and I have found this to be true in my life. I continue to be influenced by Campbell's character, and his unspoken support never went unnoticed. While he was working in Charlotte my sophomore year, Cam drove to Winston-Salem never missing a single home game. Although I rarely played, he was always there. Campbell continues to grow in his faith and has the unique ability to discern what is really important. His attention to detail, his work ethic, and his heart for others are qualities I admire—I am blessed to have a big brother like him.

Now, Campbell is married to Anne who is easy to love. Anne always brings out the best in my older brother. Her thoughtfulness never goes unnoticed. Campbell, Jr. and baby Wells continue to make me smile every time I see them.

Throughout my experiences as a walk-on, Mom was there for all of the thrilling moments. But more than anyone, my mother was there for the rough moments. So many times I remember calling mom and informing her things were not going so great. Regardless of my circumstances, her listening would evolve into responses that always seemed to point me back to the Lord—she knew where my strength came from. My mom's selflessness and sensitive nature allows her to truly love others and I am so thankful for her unconditional support throughout my life. Thanks, Mom.

Dad and I frequently shot together, so one aspect of college I disliked the most was him not being able to rebound for me. I suppose it's fitting that my dad is last on this long list because I've shared more moments in basketball with him than anyone else. He was there every step of the way. We've spent hours on the phone discussing the game, hours in the driveway shooting, and hours in the car driving to camps and tournaments. Basketball was something we loved. As much as the game meant to us, our relationship went way beyond basketball!

During my basketball career, I was always encouraged knowing there was at least one person who believed what I believed and dreamed what I dreamed. That one person was my dad and while we were driving in the car a few years ago, I told him I was going to write a book about a different perspective of college basketball. I didn't have a publisher, a cover, a chapter, or a single word—just a yellow pad with a few ideas and a possible title. I confidently told my dad, "I think I'm going to call it *Walk-On*." He believed me and today, scribbles on a yellow pad are now a book.

I don't have life perfectly mapped out, but I did find the teammate I had been looking for—the Lord brought me to Mississippi and I found her. Since the moment I first met Amanda Lynch, she has brought joy in my life that is unexplainable—joy that is much bigger than words inside a book.

"Life from the End of the Bench" to "Life with Amanda" has been a great blessing. I take comfort in knowing that wherever I now go, she'll be right beside me. I love Amanda.

I once heard that life is about relationships. The longer I live, the more I realize how true this really is. I can't imagine my life or my experiences at Wake without any of the people mentioned above. I want to say thanks for letting me be a part of all of your lives. As I approach a new season of life, I give thanks for each of you whom God has graciously used to shape my life.

I never dreamed of sitting on the bench when I was a little kid shooting hoops in the backyard, but that's the way it turned out. I am confident I was supposed to be a walk-on. There was no mistake about it. It was God's plan all along.

I remain thankful the Lord gave me the opportunity to undergo the challenges of having a "different role" because during those times I learned dependence on Christ rather than trusting in my own ability. When I wanted to quit, I found the Lord's strength in my own weakness. I learned God was more than enough for any adversity I faced, and that His grace is truly sufficient for each day.

Although I started and finished my college career on the bench, it was an experience I would never trade. It was God's "best" for me.

I press on toward the goal to win the prize
for which God has called me heavenward in Christ Jesus.
Philippians 3:14

teammates matter.™

TM

teammatesmatter.com

For more copies of this book, study guides, speaking engagement requests, or Teammates Matter™ apparel, please visit our website. Alan Williams continues to share his message of team and perseverance with various groups across the country, including corporate gatherings, schools, and other organizations. For more information, please contact info@teammatesmatter.com.